Christopher Lam

CW00967617

ORIGINAL
HONDA CB750

Other titles available in the *Original* series are:

ORIGINAL
HONDA CB750

by John Wyatt

Photography by James Mann
Edited by Cyril Ayton

Views on the jacket and preliminary pages show an
early CB750 (front cover), K6 fuel tank (half-title page),
K2 (title page), Hondamatic (contents page) and
K6 (back cover).

ACKNOWLEDGEMENTS

The author's thanks must go to Cyril Ayton who helped
at every stage, Cyd whose typing was a godsend, Alan
Taye for loan of his CB 750K2, Stuart Wilson for loan of
his CB 750K6, John Corcoran for loan of his CB 750A
and F0, Dave Ford for loan of his CB 750F1, Tim Regan
for loan of his CB 750F2, and, of course, my wife
Caroline and my children Hannah and Jodie who did
the polishing and let me keep some bikes in the kitchen.
Last but not least, of course, Rob and Chris who put up
with the shouting.

Published 1998 by Bay View Books Ltd
The Red House, 25-26 Bridgeland Street
Bideford, Devon EX39 2PZ, UK

© Copyright 1998 John Wyatt

All rights reserved. No part of this publication
may be reproduced or transmitted in any form
or by any means, electronic or mechanical,
including photocopying, recording or in
any information storage or retrieval
system, without the prior written
permission of the publisher.

Series edited by Mark Hughes
Designed by Chris Fayers

ISBN 1 901432 130
Printed in China

Contents

Introduction

The Honda CB750 became the motorcycle icon of the '70s. The bike for which the term 'superbike' was coined was certainly one of the most important motorcycles of all time. It burst on to the motorcycling scene, smashed everyone's idea of a motorcycle. Motorcycling was never the same again. Every motorcycle made since the big four's launch can trace something of its origins back to the CB750. Of course, there had been four-cylinder motorcycles before, the first one as early as 1896; and of course there had been disc brakes before, although not on a production motorcycle. But it was the whole package – the immense leap forward it represented – that had everyone gasping. Dreams became reality.

In the late '60s Honda motorcycles were, overall, the world's biggest sellers. Notably, there were the C100 Cub step-through, the biggest-selling motorbike of all time, the C71, C72, C77 and CA77/8 Dreams, and the CB72/77 Super Hawks/Sports. A glimmer of what lay ahead came with the introduction of the revolutionary CB450 dohc twin in 1966. The profits from the production bikes financed the fabulous racing machines of the '60s – and the lessons learned from racing were applied to the CB750.

In the late '60s the world's motorcycle manufacturers, the most famous and longest-established belonging to the British industry, were so complacent as to believe that the Japanese would never attempt to build a large-capacity machine. How wrong they were!

By 1972 it seemed that anywhere you went, from Los Angeles to Ankara, a CB750 was never far away, ridden by everyone from royalty to the ordinary man in the street. Honda were smart enough to realise that it would not harm sales if the rich and famous were seen on their new bike. As I write this, I can see a picture on my office wall of French film star Françoise Hardy sitting on one of the first CB750s seen in France – registered 431 W 75. I wonder where the bike is now?

The idea that Honda should build a large-capacity machine came originally from America. This was Honda's largest market, and for obvious reasons Honda wished the situation to continue. But a move upwards in capacity was needed.

There had to be a full onslaught on Triumph, BSA and Harley-Davidson territory. Some time in 1967 Bob Hansen, American Honda's service manager, had flown to Japan and discussed with Soichiro Honda the possibility of using Grand Prix technology in bikes prepared for American motorcycle events. The AMA, American racing's governing body, had rules that only allowed racing by production-based machines. Honda knew that what won on the race track today sold in the showroom tomorrow; a large-capacity road machine would have to be built in order to compete with the Triumph and Harley twins. Bob Hansen told Mr Honda that he should build a 'King of Motorcycles'.

History shows that Bob Hansen's race team blew them all away at the 1970 Daytona 200, with Dick Mann riding a tall-geared CB750 to victory. It has to be said that at this time Honda had virtually ceased all motorcycle road racing activities, attention being turned to a rather abortive first step into Grand Prix car racing; further, Honda were stepping up their efforts to become a world-class car manufacturer. All this underlines the significance of Honda's diversion of so much money and manpower to the Daytona effort. Once Daytona was won, all factory racing came to an end. The only race effort Honda then made was to supply performance kits for endurance and short-circuit racing that could be bought by privateers. These kits, though, were prohibitively expensive and usually only purchased by importers or very large dealers.

CB750 made the Honda name familiar to thousands of sports bike riders in the late '60s.

'Honda were smart enough to realise that it would not harm sales if the rich and famous were seen on their new bike.' Singer Françoise Hardy, CB750, Paris – a shot borrowed from the author's office wall...

There was nothing 'flash' about the 750's self advertising – 'OHC 750' cast into the cam box was about as flamboyant as Honda got.

The first disc brake fitted to a production motorcycle: CB750's 11.7in diameter unit was a revelation to riders in the late '60s.

The Prototypes

I have not managed to find out how many prototype CB750s were produced but I do know that some were made with a front drum brake and a CB450-type fuel tank. These, I believe, were the first to be made in the metal, and looked very much like the final production bike. The exhaust system was of the four-into-four type, although the silencers were not seamed and looked like those later fitted to the CB750 K7. A later prototype I have seen looked even more like the final model; I am sure this was the last prototype before the design was finalised, though it had tyres that resembled trials knobblies! However, the front mudguard was almost the same as the production type. Strangely, the fork top yoke had very set-back handlebar clamps which put the bars about 2in behind the line of the front forks. It is amusing to think that after-market suppliers made so much money from producing 'Set Backs', which sold like hot cakes in America to people who were short in the arm or wanted to be more comfortable behind a fairing. The prototype also had twin horns – not featured on the production machines.

The fuel tank on the one I have seen was indistinguishable from the production item, being painted in gold with K2-style black stripes and trim. The side covers were larger than the production ones and curved down at the bottom nearly to the level of the swing arm spindle. These had odd badges, with a Honda wing in a circular centre with two extensions either side. I think these said '750 FOUR'. The centre stand had three legs for stability, which was unusual if not unique. It did not reach production. Switches were from the CB450, and had a pol-

ished finish instead of being satin black. The engine, at this time, was of the same general layout as the production version but I doubt that any part would fit a production engine. It looked very much like the engines shown at the 1968 Tokyo show with 'pumper' type CR carburettors and totally different outer covers. I don't know if it had the crankcase top clutch mechanism, which was changed, for production, to a set-up hidden behind the chrome plate on the clutch cover. The most significant part of the bike was the air box, which was in black and seemed to have been strengthened, to stop it cracking. It was a shame that this took so long to reach production.

Many collectors have tried to locate some of these pre-production machines, and I have to say that some have created their own! I only know of one genuine version. We weren't able to photograph it because it is being restored.

I would like to have devoted more time to digging up interesting facts for this section, but photographs and information are unfortunately hard to find, and without factory help it has been difficult to establish even this scant background.

A precursor of the CB750: revolutionary CB450 dohc twin of 1966. This machine displayed high tech at almost every point – not least in employing torsion bar valve springs.

The Times: Late '60s, Early '70s

I remember very well the launch of the Honda CB750 at the Tokyo Show of October 1968 and the Brighton Show of April 1969: headlines were all over the motorcycle press of the day. My favoured bike at the time was a Bridgestone 350GTR which seemed a fantastic machine to someone who a year or two earlier had been riding around on a bicycle. Sure enough, it wasn't long before the big boys in my neck of the tarmac had traded in their Tritons, Beezas and Bonnevilles for the latest Hondas and were to be seen outside the café on a Friday and Saturday night. I think it was the colour that grabbed me most, or maybe the four chromed pipes. I'm sure most enthusiasts remember their first sighting, and sound...

My first acquaintance with the CB750 was at second hand, reading David Dixon's write-up on the bike in the weekly *Motor Cycle* in the summer of '69. I recall (actually I've looked it up) his writing... 'A tiny electric-starter button by the twistgrip growls the 67 horses into life... The experience starts...heaviness and bulk [are] forgotten within the first few yards. The bike is beautifully balanced. A combination of complete smoothness and effortless torque waft you up to the nineties so rapidly...'

David was riding the Honda on the 14.2-mile Nürburgring GP circuit. He found the notorious curves and corners, descents and climbs brought out the bike's 'racing background'. The power and speed of the 750 – 118mph at 8000rpm, with over 125mph predicted in better conditions – got high marks from D.D., while handling also came in for praise. And that perhaps was not entirely expected for it was gospel in those far-off days that the Brits were the only people who could build bikes with ace steering. But Dixon wrote: 'Front and rear suspension are well matched with rebound damping firm enough to prevent the wallowing and bouncing so often associated with Japanese bikes...sharp undulations chucked the machine well clear of the road [at over 100mph], yet directional stability remained bang on, with scarcely a nod from the steering head...the Honda four ranks as one of the most outstanding machines I have ever ridden.'

Whew. You'll perhaps appreciate why I

decided early on that I had to have one of these CB750s...

Later I got to know more of the man who penned those enthusiastic words during his years as boss of Dixon Racing Ltd in Surrey when he imported from Japan a wide range of superb-quality go-faster CB750 componentry made by tuner 'Pops' Yoshimura. Twenty years on, nobody produces a more effective race kit for Japanese motorcycles than 'Pops' turned out for the CB750 in its day.

Extra value, I believe, belongs to write-ups which appear when the object of praise – or disgust! – is new. You can't accuse the writer of hindsight. Even more influential than David Dixon in firing and maintaining my enthusiasm for the big Honda were the writings of M.R.W. – he was identified only by initials – published in the monthly *Motorcycle Sport* magazine. M.R.W. (Mark Ramsey Wigan, as I learned later) had bought one of the earliest CB750s imported into the UK. He had much to say, almost all of it good, about his new bike. In June 1970 he described his first miles on 'Pheidippides': 'My new Honda CB750 earned its name scant miles from the Oxford showrooms of Bill Faulkner, who supplied it. My Bridgestone 350GTR has gone. The 350 gave me a wonderful run up to Oxford when

The heart shared by all the CB750 variants covered in this book – the magnificent four-cylinder single overhead camshaft engine. It is seen in a very early model from 1969.

Early CB750 owner's manual: well-written and translated (true!), and now a rare item on an autojumble table. It's big, which means it won't fit into the handbook holder designed to fit under the seat of later models.

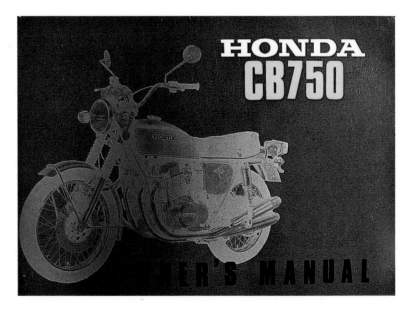

getting the Honda. As 102mph came up on the clock in fifth, and I changed up to top gear, I had momentary qualms about letting it go. Still, it has gone, and the next owner will have the pleasure of discovering just how quickly it can accelerate. Indeed, the Honda Four is little quicker to 70mph, though the Honda's acceleration curve keeps going steeply up to about 105mph and then begins to tail off.

'Running-in is fairly extended for the plain-bearing Four, and little serious throttle bending could be expected for a thousand miles or more. The first few of these miles were a delightful relief: with only one-eighth throttle, the limit of 4000rpm imposed for the first few hundred miles was hardly a limitation, as this allowed up to 60mph in top gear. The flexibility was exemplary,

and the low-speed handling of the big machine was extremely light and positive. As a result, the 40 miles home were gone in a very short time, and the comfortable and long-legged pace of the 750 showed it to be a real marathon runner. Pheidippides was the original runner who came back to Athens bearing the news of Marathon (he then, poor fellow, died on arrival having passed on his message). The name was not yet earned, however, and the running-in miles rolled by. The 600-mile mark was reached, and maximum rpm was then raised slowly to 6000 (95mph in top gear) by the 1000-mile point.

'By this time minor irritations had begun to show up, and familiarity lent a sharper blade to my critical faculties. The footbrake pedal was non-adjustable, and about ¾in too high; the kickstart

Superb styling of the early CB750 was never bettered throughout the 10-year series. The appealing colour is Candy Blue-Green.

lever rubbed uncomfortably against my right leg, the lower gears had a crunchy BMW-like feel, requiring great deliberation for a satisfactory low-speed change into first or second gears. Last, and far from least, a small oil seepage could be seen round the cylinder head. This appeared to come not from the gasket but from the two O-rings on the oil path feeding the head under pressure. I have seen several 750s with the same seepage, including one of French origin. I am not at all pleased with oil leaks of any kind, and the results of this slow, steady seepage were visible on the air filter covers by this time. I hope that a cure for this irritant can be found: it is still only an irritant, but it is one that has no place on this otherwise extremely clean machine.

'A more surprising event was the failure of not one but three rear-lamp filaments in the first 1500 miles. The rear lamp unit is mounted on a rubber mat, so it is evident that high-frequency vibrations can be expected to affect the bulbs, but the very faint tremors and minor vibrations detectable by the rider would seem to make bulb failure a very unlikely occurrence. However, the evidence is there; vibrate it does.

'While on the negative line, another unfavourable comment: the steering and handling of the 750 are both excellent, but when panniers, pillion passenger and other luggage is aboard, a steering wobble is evident between 40 and 60mph – this can only be found by waiting for a bump in the road and removing both hands from the bars, and is in no sense dangerous.

'The front fork lower yoke is cast with an attachment point for a hydraulic damper unit, and indeed one is listed among the production racing components homologated for the model. One hopes that (at least) a token number of such original Honda components will find their way on to the shelves of Honda (UK's) parts store rooms.

'Too often have other manufacturers – nearer home – failed to make available such components used to gain notable victories for the factory: it is sadly true that the more successful is the manufacturer in the production racing field, the more necessary it becomes to make the special parts

This CB750 is a restored bike but it features all original parts, apart from the exhaust. Representing the model in its earliest form, it features at length in this book.

available to the public in order to bolster the credibility of the results. Production racing is a strongly supported class, and surely it is worthwhile establishing the close links with the ordinary product? If such steps are not taken, the normal (and natural) conclusion is drawn that the links are not as close as the advertisers would have one believe, notwithstanding the truth of the unfavourable economics that usually apply to the sale of such equipment.

'The brakes are highly unlikely ever to attract such commentary: not only is the standard single disc at the front one of the most powerful and fade-free brakes I have used, but a twin-disc layout can be installed merely by purchasing a second set of standard brake components, and fitting them to the positions already cast in on the right-hand side. The caliper mounting is symmetric, and the caliper itself can be fitted straight on in the 180 degrees opposed position. The *sole* 'special' part is a double hose connector at the junction of the high-pressure hoses on the lower fork yoke,

M.R.W., writing in *Motorcycle Sport*, found the CB750 was good for 120mph and 48-52mpg. It was, he wrote, '...a very satisfactory machine, an excellent tourer, and usable on a race track'.

M.R.W. on the early CB750's landmark front disc set-up: '...one of the most powerful and fade-free brakes I have used...'

although the caliper mounting arm might require some attention to obtain the correct 'zero' positioning. Such a modification would not be unduly cheap, but at least all the parts are readily available.' (*In hindsight, M.R.W. was wrong. Fitting twin discs to a 750 calls for some ingenuity in accommodating the front mudguard bracket and speedo drive.*)

'In everyday use the disc brake soon becomes familiar, and the simple relationship of squeeze harder, stop quicker applies right up to tyre-smoking stops from 60mph.

'The Honda is a heavy bike – 517lb (wet) – but the weight transfer under braking is so complete that the rear brake can be used only very lightly indeed. In the course of ten runs of 0-100mph-0, carried out without pause, no fade was apparent.

'This hydraulic braking system has been criticised for lack of lever adjustment. This is actually based on a lack of information; there is ample provision for adjustment by a neat grub screw arrangement at the lever pivot. It is not immediately apparent, but is soon found if one suspects

that it should be there! The neat handlebar-mounted master cylinder for the front brake operates perfectly well when re-installed at a steep angle: there is, therefore, no difficulty inherent in using Ace-style bars to obtain a riding position better fitted to high-speed riding. The manuals refer to 'SAE J 1703a' brake fluid for the American market: Honda (UK) tell us that Girling Crimson is the correct hydraulic fluid to use.

'The 12in disc is stainless steel and has remained corrosion-free over the first 1500 miles, many of which were carried out in very wet conditions. Unfortunately the inside face is already showing minor scores; these are at present within the 0.012in tolerance allowed by Honda, but for noticeable wear to occur in such a short mileage is not exactly encouraging.

'The action of this type of brake gives one far more control over the actual retarding force as the more normal leading/trailing shoe-actuated systems all rely on self-servo action to a greater or lesser extent: this inevitably reduces the range of hand pressures over which strong retardation can

be produced, and increases the chances of wheel-locking. On the debit side the hydraulic brake does not help the hand with any servo action, and therefore requires a really strong squeeze for the full braking power to be developed.

'When changing the high, wide and handsome standard handlebars for a spare pair of CB450 bars as a temporary trial, it was apparent that the high-pressure hose for the brake fluid would be the cause of considerable awkwardness if any narrower straight bars were required, unless one was prepared to strip the hose. It was interesting to note that the handlebar control clips now have locating pegs that stop these units from slowly rotating round the bars. The sheer number of electrical cables that had to be teased through the hollow handlebars make me very reluctant to change the bars back again, having at last sorted it all out correctly!

'The headlamp of the CB750 is conveniently of 7in diameter and is fitted with a 35/35 watt bulb. This is quite inadequate for the performance available. I have fitted a 7in Cibié unit with 40/45

Introduced in 1971, the K2 brought many refinements to the original CB750 design and went on to be a big seller. The colour of this one is Planet Blue metallic custom.

Notable changes incorporated in the K6 included an endless (ie, without spring link) rear chain, a more comfortable seat and bolder styling. The colour of this one is Candy Antarese red.

watt filaments as a temporary measure, until a dipping quartz-iodine unit (of Lucas origin) arrives. The extra range and intensity of the Cibié is greatly appreciated, although it is only fair to report that 60mph could be maintained with the standard unit.

'The mounting arrangements are worth a comment. The glass and reflector unit is mounted in a 7in rim, and retained by a flat-pressed metal ring that locates *and* retains the reflector in exactly the right location without any of those infernal 'W' clips. This rim is connected to a false rim by two screws which locate the unit on a vertical diameter. The third locating point is by a spring-loaded screw at the right-hand edge of the false rim. This arrangement makes alignment, replacement and alteration to the headlamp extremely easy and commendably exact.

'This sort of detail can be found all over the machine when one looks closely at it: it is abundantly clear that Honda have really done their best for this model, in spite of an incredibly short design and development period of less than a year

from first thoughts to the American market. Unfortunately everyone must have kept well out of the way of the test riders, as the horn looks nice, but is really only decorative. A bull-lunged klaxon would really be an asset to the 750, as it is too quiet and too fast for anything else to be of any real value. It is possible to flash up the head beam, due to the arrangement of the light switch.

'On the French model a neat extra control is fitted: this is a single switch with 'Day' and 'Night' settings. On 'Day' the horn button acts on the horn, but on the 'Night' setting the horn button acts as a normal headlamp flasher. I wonder at the legality of this arrangement in the UK: don't the rules say that a horn must be in working order? If such a switch were fitted to the *starter* button, however…perhaps Honda (UK) could consider the idea when specifying future UK models in the top price bracket?

'The Honda is most deceptively sleek, and nothing hangs outside an (approximate) 50 degrees vee when the stands are removed; even with the stands in place there is only a degree or

two less available. This means that even with passenger and luggage nothing 'decks' except the toes of the unwary pillion rider who lets his shoes point down too far.

'It takes quite a few miles to realise how well the Honda goes round corners; it is only the angle of the horizon as you start to come back up that lets you know! Japanese tyre compounds and treads have really improved. I have no complaints about the standard tyres in dry weather, but still some reservations about them in the wet. My usual swift recourse to Dunlop or Avon before racing has been delayed to give the Japanese Dunlops (FJ and K87) a thorough trial, although the rim sizes of WM2 and 3 take available K81 Dunlops. The inferior wet-road adhesion is probably due mainly to the details of the Japanese compound as the central region tread pattern is very similar to K81: my major complaint is that the tread simply doesn't go far enough round the tyre!

I have abraded the last thou of tread pattern without grounding anything yet, so K81s are the obvious next move.

'As I write, the Four has over 1500 miles on the clock, and short bursts of up to 8500rpm have been used. No real attempt has been made so far to obtain full performance. Three swift gear changes at 8000rpm leave one neatly at 100mph, and on one occasion the revs were allowed to rise to give 108mph before shutting off: the machine was still accelerating, and I had made no attempts at all to crouch down behind the handlebars!

'I hope to determine a reasonable 'maximile' speed at Snetterton, and get a fair idea of the performance available. As I ride to and from meetings, I have no intention of doing any more than enjoy myself at my own (uncompetitive) rate. The Honda bids fair to meet my three major requirements:

1. To give me a good ride in production races.

In 1975 Honda pepped up the CB750 range by adding the Super Sport model, with revised styling (especially for the fuel tank), a little more engine power and a four-into-one exhaust. Examples shown are F0 (above) and F1 (facing page). Note the very neat, practical engine crash bars which saved many expensive crankcases from damage.

2. To carry large loads with good grace and over long distances.

3. To provide a speedy, manageable and good-handling machine for pure enjoyment, which includes quick trips to and through the metropolis.

'Requirement 1 will be tested shortly, requirement 2 has been fully met, and a weekend spent in Lincolnshire was the occasion. The 200 miles were covered at a steady 70-80mph, at a small throttle opening into a very strong wind: both rider and passenger were very comfortable on the well-designed seat at the end of the run. The sheer lack of fatigue was a great improvement over most of the other machines that I have ridden, and the passenger's point of view is best expressed by the occasion on which I was told worriedly: "It's vibrating!" (I had, in fact, used 7500rpm when pulling away from a petrol station, and a slight vibration period exists near 6000rpm.) On further

enquiry I learnt that *no* vibration had been felt up to that time, in spite of much swift overtaking and running between 60 and 80 plus.

'This good touring behaviour is not spoilt by unduly high petrol consumption: I have returned 48-52mpg over the last 1500 miles, doing 49mpg over the whole 450-mile weekend referred to. I could do considerably better, but like to use a good part of the swift acceleration available.

'A really nice feature of the Honda's handling is that it holds its line accurately over bumps and ripples taken at speed: the heavy-duty swinging arm is fully up to the job in a way that the CB77's never was. The clutch is also a great improvement over earlier Hondas: it is light and positive; the throw-out mechanism being particularly neat. Three balls are held in a triangular cage, and the clutch lever operates an arm that causes these balls to roll up a ramp, thereby pushing the clutch disengagement rod inwards. The throw-out rod

acts on a cup in the centre of a ballrace, so that the clutch can be held out for a long period if necessary without ill-effects. This clutch, otherwise very satisfactory, produces an alarming clatter at low (tickover) speeds, as if all the plates were juddering back and forth on the clutch plate splines. This is unfortunate, as this is the loudest noise that can be heard when the machine is ticking over at under 1000rpm. At least it is not as obtrusive as the deafening rattle produced by the 350 Bridgestone's dry clutch!

'The exhaust silencing is excellent, and the rider only notices the exhaust when the revs rise above about 5500rpm, when the wailing exhaust note can begin to be heard. I have not often had occasion to hear someone else pass by on a Four, but when I have the note is a beautiful reminder of the hollow howl of the racing six.

'We really must find some new way of discussing vibration: all the new multi-cylinder machines have some faint vibrations, but when compared to the smoothest of two-strokes or four-stroke singles there's nothing significant to be felt. I had the opportunity to swap machines with a Velocette Viper rider on my trip to Lincolnshire:

this Velocette was in really excellent condition and very 'smooth'. Yet, changing from Four to single, both the owner of the Viper and I noted the considerable vibration of the single.

'One interesting point is that Honda specifies 95 octane (or above) for the CB750 (9:1 compression ratio), which is two stars less than the BSA/Triumph threes seem to need!

'The main design limitation of the Four would seem to be the final drive chain. The torque and power that are put through this unprotected chain could be expected to enforce frequent chain readjustments. In practice no adjustment has proved necessary over the last 1000 miles, after the first bedding-in and a subsequent thorough cleaning and Linklyfeing. Part of this good behaviour is due to the neat and simple chain-oiling system. A shallow spill way picks up a small amount of oil, and leads to a hole in the centre of the final drive sprocket. The oil is then thrown by centrifugal force outward across the face of the sprocket on to the chain. This metering system seems both to keep the chain lightly oiled and to avoid pools of oil on the garage floor.

'The adjustment of the chain is simple and

If earlier F series models had lacked a little in presence, the purposeful F2 (above) of 1977 changed all that – twin front discs, black-painted engine, Comstar wheels, single, large megaphone-style silencer.

Hondamatic (facing page), also seen in 1977 guise, was not so strong on enthusiast appeal, but its two-speed automatic transmission gave some touring advantages.

rapid, aided by the positioning marks on the rear forks. The removal of the rear wheel is an equally pleasant occupation. The front wheel is simple to remove, but woe betide the unwary who touch the brake lever when the wheel is out: a full brake re-bleeding will then be necessary.

'After the previous part of the road test report had been written, the Honda was ridden at Snetterton during several of the races run by the Southern Sixty Seven Racing Club. I rode the machine the 140 miles to the track in precisely standard trim barring the slightly lower CB450 handlebars. The Honda was then raced on the Japanese tyres, and indeed all else was just as delivered from the showroom. The speedometer was calibrated on the way, and at a steady 70mph the actual speed was 69mph – surprisingly accurate. Indeed, the indicated road speed at all rpm in top corresponded with the value calculated from the gearing. Being of cautious vein, and of fragile pocket since purchasing the CB750, I was in no great hurry to prove anything: the object of the exercise was to give the Honda a thorough performance test, excluding cornering heroics on tyres with tread insufficiently far round the tyre walls.

'Acceleration was excellent, and on the grand-stand straight 100-105mph could be obtained before braking for Riches Corner. On the first lap of the last race I was starting to use the front brake really hard with more confidence and control, but made the error of using the rear as much (or rather as little) as before: as a result the bike hopped all over the place, as if it had an oily rear tyre. A wide excursion while examining the rear lost a good four seconds before the obvious penetrated. This minor incident really brought home to me the extent of the weight transfer to the front wheel on heavy braking, as I was hardly touching the rear brake pedal.

'Not being able to use full lean (due to lack of tread on Japanese tyres), and not really wishing to, the only handling comments I can make are that there was some weaving on the ripples of both Riches and the entry to the Norwich Straight. A pair of beautiful Velocettes came whistling past through Sears Corner, canted over at least 15 degrees more than a timorous MRW: as we went up the straight the Honda was catching them up quite easily, but seconds gained on the straights were scant help! Stronger damping at the rear would help, but for all other use the Japnitrogens were fine. The 750 accelerated rapidly up to 100-102 in fourth, and then up to 110 in fifth: the last 5-6mph came more slowly, but had I entered the straight more quickly about another 2-3mph were left, by my estimation. This top speed of 120-121 corresponded to about 8400rpm, just under the red line, and 400rpm over the top of peak power.

Ronald Baylie's Four – which came in the first four in both Production races – was rather quicker, and was pulling 8500 on a 43-tooth rear sprocket (two down from standard), corresponding to just under 130mph.

'The braking from 120mph was first essayed at the 300-yard marker, but this was very quickly found to be too early: by the end of the day my braking point was at about the 200-yard marker. I did 80 miles on the track that day, and at the end of the day 120-121mph was coming up just as reliably as at the beginning and no brake fade had been noted. This was not surprising, as I was still slowly and steadily increasing the maximum braking force that I was exacting at the close. A measure of the sedateness of my ride is that my lap speeds lay firmly in the range 76-78mph and that I finished 14th and 12th in the two production races that day.

'This performance by the Honda, ably sabotaged by my timorous riding, fully satisfies my condition (1). With K81 tyres fitted (*when* I have worn out the Japanese) I intend to have a more serious 'go' on the track. An interesting point about the 'feel' of the bike is that it never felt 'heavy' and even at the quick left-right bends little effort was needed.

'After the races, the stands went back on, the winkers refitted and the tape removed from the lights. The tank was refilled and the fuel consumption turned out at 36mpg for all that maximum rpm riding.

'A delightful 120-mile ride back home ensued, which returned the 'usual' 49mpg for 70-plus travelling and enthusiastic use of the acceleration. On the open roads beyond Newmarket an Elan came past out of a corner and, sitting bolt upright, I and the Elan levelled off at 111mph from the start of 70 for me and rather more for him. We maintained station. Above 80 the aerodynamics of two wheels are appalling and with rider bolt upright are worse: this brief encounter showed that the Honda-type pressure recommendations (above 175kph/110mph use 32-34 psi) are actually necessary for riders with machines in complete standard trim: bars and all.

'To sum up these (now 2000-mile) impressions… A very satisfactory machine: an excellent tourer, usable on a race track and probably very competitive in the right hands, very good low-speed handling and flexibility – it will snap away from 2000rpm in fifth – but with one or two niggling blemishes. It is under-tyred, being a little skittish in the wet, and can lean more than the tread allows (I have abraded the tread a little to the edge of the pattern without grounding), reasonably economical even when fair use is made of the performance, and a quiet, tractable and light-handling motorcycle with a solid and sure feel.'

CB750s have been author John Wyatt's meat and drink ever since he bought his K2 in 1974 (top). He went on to do 25,000 almost trouble-free miles on it in all weathers. He still rides CB750s (above) and restores them for a living (right), although his 'phone number has changed since he did this one.

Over the years, I don't think I've ever read a better account than that of the CB750's many virtues, and few drawbacks.

It wasn't long before the hard men (or would-be hard men) on their Norton Commandos, 500 Kawasakis, T500 Suzukis, BSA Rocket 3s, Yamaha YR5s *and 750 Hondas* were all mixing it together around our local roads. The Rocket 3s were a little faster than the Honda, and possibly handled slightly better. The Kawasakis were perhaps the most fun. The Suzukis were reliable, but thirsty and bland. Commandos and YR5s were the best handlers. But it was only when the summer got into its stride and trips to all the race meetings meant that everybody was doing some serious miles, plenty of them flat-out on the M1, that the real champion stood out. The Rocket 3s sometimes blew up, and invariably still leaked oil, like their predecessors – *if* the electrics stayed alive long enough for you to get them hot. The Norton Commandos blew up, too, between problems such as electrics failing, gearboxes seizing and parts falling off at random, although I have to say that about one in 100 seemed to stay together regardless of treatment. The Kawasaki's prodigious thirst, not only for fuel and oil but pistons as well, could begin to overshadow the fun factor. The Suzuki was still only a 500 two-stroke twin and seemed to fall between two stools: on the one hand it was small and agile, but then you always felt you had to ride it very hard to keep the others in sight on a long run. The YR5, a 350, was just too small for these distances, getting blown about and having to be held flat-out to keep up with the larger machines, thus losing any advantage in nimbleness. And these proud owners couldn't help but notice that the Honda just kept on going, all day, up hill, down dale, and when they all finally returned to the café it would be the Honda that sat there ticking over, as if it had just been round the block. In short, it was almost 100% reliable, keenly priced – and easily available from a plethora of dealers world-wide.

When you had spent just about all your money in buying your bike, this in-built reliability was a bonus indeed. All you really needed to do was fill it up and change the oil at regular intervals. That is not to say you didn't need to keep a wary eye on the drive chain and find some money now and again for a rear tyre, but then you had to do that with most bikes. You could happily set off on a journey of almost any length without doing any preparatory maintenance whatsoever – a real novelty! Except, of course, for those many riders who had been brought up on Honda reliability with the firm's earlier, smaller, bikes. Speaking for myself, I finally swapped a Volkswagen Beetle for a K2 750 in 1974 and went on to do 25,000 almost trouble-free miles on it in all weathers.

This was a wonderful period for motorcycling. With a reliable motorcycle, the whole country was opened up to me in the way it was, I presume, to all the others who now felt confident in undertaking any kind of trip, in any kind of weather. Finally car-type reliability had come to bikes and the face of motorcycling had probably changed for everyone, forever. Not everyone, though, was as taken with the CB750 as I was. The old school of extremely conservative motorcyclists, most of whom had to spend hours tinkering with their machines before they felt they were enjoying their motorcycling, had plenty to say about this new upstart: "Too complicated"…"Jap crap"… "Won't last five minutes". I notice most of these fellows tend to ride around on VFR 750s these days, and swear by them!

Most of my trips were made between eastern England and the north-west over the Pennine range, which is notorious for the foulest of weather. These rides were undertaken in all seasons, and although enjoyable bend-swinging was to be had during the summer months some horrendous trips were endured in winter. One particular effort that stands out in my mind was from Carlisle to Wetherby via the A66, then a tortuous road. Setting off one Sunday evening from Carlisle at 5pm, I encountered snow on the M6 about 10 miles south of Carlisle, and as I turned on to the A66 blizzard conditions set in and continued from Penrith to Scotch Corner. The A66 goes straight over the top of the Pennines and can catch travellers out in the best of weather. Twenty-five years ago this road was extremely challenging, with every type of corner and camber; if you were going to travel quickly, serious concentration was required. Unfortunately the road has since been improved, to the extent that it has lost its character, and is now nearly all dual-carriageway. When the authorities have outlawed all cars, I hope they will return such roads to how they used to be, for enthusiasts to enjoy again!

As I progressed eastward along the A66 the weather got worse and worse, and the road effectively ceased to exist. Wind whipped up the snow to drifts about 6ft high on my left. The big question at these times is always 'Do I turn back?' or 'Do I go on?' Being a reckless optimist, I carried on. The road had by now disappeared completely and I was climbing higher, where I knew it would be even colder. My only clues to the direction of the road were the poles on the left-hand side indicating the height of the snow drifts. Only about 18in of these 8ft poles was still visible. I found if I kept going at 45mph, with both feet on the footrests, progress could be maintained. As in all these situations, reserves, physical and mental, seem to be automatically brought into play, and what were extremely treacherous road conditions

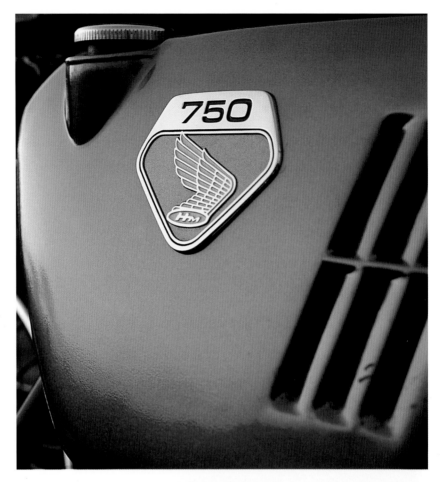

began to seem almost normal. It was at this moment, at the summit of Stainmoor, that I realised I could not feel my hands or feet and that hypothermia was probably just starting to set in. Would I make it to Scotch Corner, or was I destined to remain forever in one of the loneliest spots in Britain? The polar explorer Robert Swan, after all, lives here as it reminds him of the barren wastes of the Arctic! Only determination to get to the warmth of home kept me going. As the

Compared with British bikes of the period, the CB750 scored on style, integrating vital components into the overall lines of a motorcycle. There was even a shapely cover (top) to conceal the dry-sump oil tank.

OUTLINE SPECIFICATION AT LAUNCH, 1968

Price	$1295 (USA), £679 19s (UK)
Kerb weight	517lb
Frame	Double cradle in tubular steel
Suspension	
front	Telescopic fork
rear	Swinging arm
Tyres	
front	3.25×19in (4pr)
rear	4.00×18in (4pr)
Brakes	
front	11.7in disc
rear	7in drum
Fuel tank capacity	5 US gallons, 4 imperial gallons, 18 litres
Engine type	SOHC air-cooled in-line four-cylinder
Bore and stroke	2.401×2.480in, 61×63mm
Displacement	44.93cu in, 736 cc
Compression ratio	9.0:1
Carburettors	4 Keihin, piston-valve type
Maximum power	67PS @ 8000rpm
Maximum torque	44.12lb ft @ 7000rpm, 6.1kgm @ 7000rpm
Oil tank capacity	7.4 US pints, 6.2 imperial pints, 3.5 litres
Lubrication	Forced pressure; dry sump
Engine weight	176.3lb, 80kg (including oil)
Clutch	Multi-plate type
Transmission	Five-speed constant-mesh
Primary reduction	1.708:1
Secondary reduction	1.167:1
Internal gear ratios	First 2.500:1; second 1.708:1; third 1.333:1; fourth 1.097:1; fifth 0.939:1
Final reduction	2.812:1
Maximum speed	125mph, 200kph
Fuel consumption	40-60mpg
Braking	32ft from 30mph

Early CB750 'sand-cast' crankcase has rougher finish than later die-cast case.

downhill stretch to Scotch Corner approached so the cold worsened. However, I made it to Scotch Corner and pulled into the small petrol station next to the hotel. The whole of the right-hand side of the bike was white. I couldn't even see through the wire-spoke wheels. As I filled up, the near-frozen petrol pump attendant, dressed in what can only be described as 'severe weather' clothing, said "Where have you come from?" "Carlisle," I replied. "How have you got here from there?" he asked. "On the A66," I replied. "But it's been closed since midday, like all the other cross-Pennine routes north of here. You must be mad!" I probably was. That small experience, in essentials shared with thousands of other motorcyclists caught in inclement weather, might have ended tragically if the bike hadn't been so totally dependable.

When the desire to race came with a change of machine, I never forgot the enjoyment to be had from a reliable bike which let you get on with the delight of riding. I have owned one or another CB750 model since 1983, as well as making my living by professionally restoring them for enthusiasts since 1988. I have to add here that my trips to and from Carlisle happened only once a fortnight; on the 'spare' weekend, I used to spend Sunday cleaning the bike and lubing the rear chain, this being about the level of my abilities at the time. My friends used to call and berate me for doing this, but I enjoyed it. Apart from having to rebuild the spokes in the rear wheel, and change numerous rear chains and tyres, I only did the maintenance as set out in the hand book.

People today complain of the CB750's exhaust system, which has always been expensive, rotting from the inside. Mine never did, and I believe the reason was that I cleaned the outside of the system once a month in winter and that I never subjected the bike to short runs, which would fail to purge the exhausts of condensation. Another interesting fact about these times was that most owners threw away their original tyres almost from day one. The power of the press had brainwashed everyone into thinking that Japanese Dunlops and Bridgestones were rubbish. A fellow CB750 owner, local to myself, bought up as many of these tyres as he could. Some people gave them to him or sold them at little cost. It seems strange that he was the fastest of the local riders, the only one who could scrape the alternator cover on the road. Most owners of the day fitted Dunlop TT100 tyres, which were hailed as the tyres to have, but I don't believe the CB750 was suited to the TT100's trigonic tread section, and today I would always suggest a Metzeler ME11 front and ME77 rear in the standard sizes as the best all-round tyres for the CB750. One bonus is that the Metzeler tread pattern is similar to that of the originals.

Engine & Transmission

Engine

No matter how impressive the whole bike was on its first appearance, it was, of course, the 750's engine that grabbed most attention. A four-cylinder across the frame, with single overhead camshaft, all aluminium, it had a bore and stroke of 61×63mm, which made it just 'under-square', and the capacity was 736cc. The crankcase was horizontally split at the centre line of the crank-shaft, countershaft and mainshaft, and additionally housed oil pump and filter, kick-starter gear, selector drum and shaft, primary chain tensioner and final drive shaft. It was an extremely robust crankcase and to the best of my knowledge never needed strengthening even when used, as often happened, in drag racing and other competition applications. The first 7414 engines built had crankcases that were gravity die-cast, as opposed to the pressure die-casting of all later sohc vari-

What a great-looking engine! Fin-less oil filter bowl and 'sand-cast' crankcase indicate an early CB750.

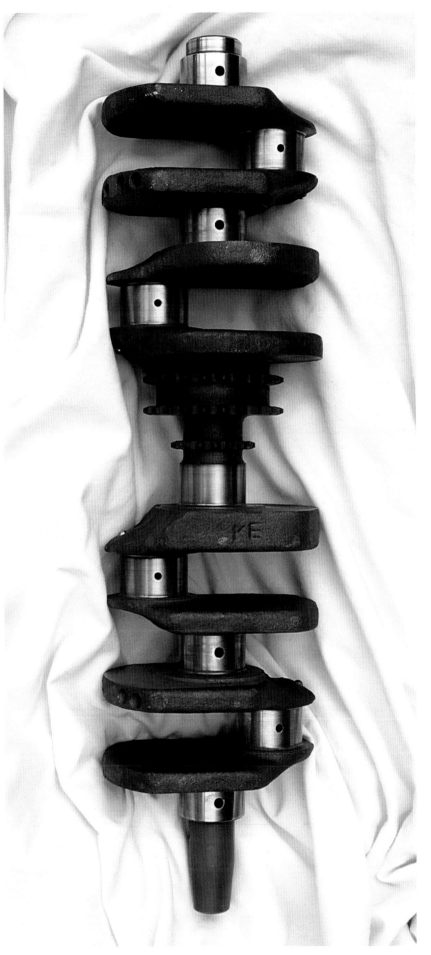

ants. The 'gravity' versions can be easily spotted by their rough finish. On top of the crankcase went the one-piece cylinder assembly, topped by the one-piece cylinder head.

The crankshaft departed from normal Honda practice in that it was a one-piece forging, not pressed together. Naturally, then, plain bearings were used for mains and big ends. There were five main bearings.

The left-hand end of the crankshaft was tapered, driving the electric starter's ring gear and the alternator rotor (of which more later). The rotor was attached by a large bolt threaded into the tapered end of the crankshaft. The bolt was changed to a larger size at engine number CB 750E-1001081. All the torque settings I have seen for this bolt are 72.3lb ft; however, if you have an early bike with the smaller bolt, beware – it will snap if torqued to this figure. The right-hand end was cut short and had a threaded 6mm shaft (with an O-ring screwed into it) which, using a hole in the crankshaft end for location, drove the

Crankshaft is supported in five main bearings. Details show peened-over ball sealing oil gallery (top) and markings that denote journal sizes (above).

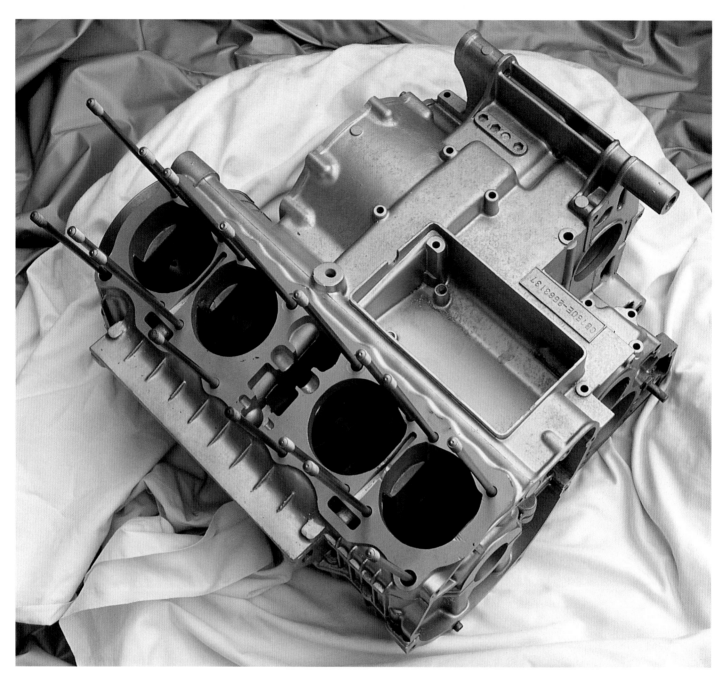

advancer assembly and the contact-breaker points, of which there were two. The oil galleries in the crankshaft were drilled and sealed by set screws at first, then later by peened-over balls.

Connecting rods were forged and had split caps held together by special bolts and nuts. The gudgeon pins ran directly in the small end eye. If there was a weak point in the engine, the connecting rods were probably the one that stood out, certainly in tuned versions, although I have never known a con rod fail in a standard engine. There were three sets of teeth integral with the crankshaft; one drove the cam chain, and to the right the other pair drove the double primary chain set.

The selection of bearing shells was interesting in that on the underside of the front of the top crankcase were stamped five letters, one for each

CB750 crankcase, seen from two angles – cylinder bore measures 61mm.

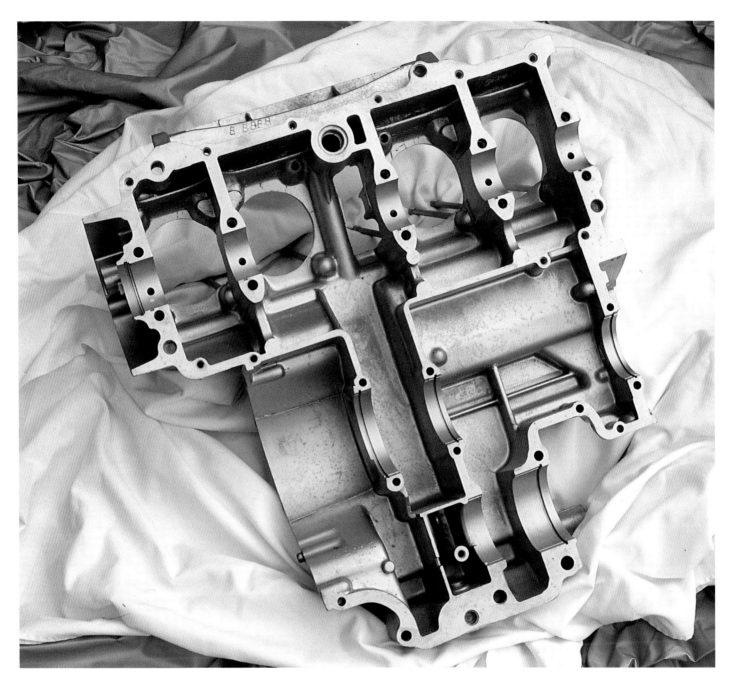

Top crankcase from the same bike is also seen stripped and cleaned for inspection. These components are from a K6, on which cylinder studs vary.

crankcase journal, A or B (eg, AAAAB or BBBAB, etc). The procedure was to write these down and then look at the crankshaft, which on the flywheel face closest to the primary chain sprockets would have etched on it – for example – JL-AABBC PL-3434 with J (for journal), L (meaning read from the left), -AABBC P (for pin) and L (meaning read from the left) -3434. The first five letters, ignoring the J and L, that's to say, AABBC, you then also wrote down, and compared with a chart in the workshop manual. This gave you the correct shells for each journal. The four numbers 3434 related to the con rods. You noted these and had a look at each con rod, on which there were two markings: a letter, which was the weight code and was to be ignored in this instance, and a number which you corresponded

with the one on the crankshaft, and checked against a chart in the manual.

Unusually among late '60s bikes, the CB750's engine was of dry sump type, with a separate oil tank connected to the engine by two flexible pipes, one for oil delivery and one for return. These were attached to the lower right-hand side of the crankcase by flanges built into the pipes and held to the case by two bolts per flange. Short oil galleries led to the oil pump mounted, by three bolts, to the bottom of the lower crankcase. This arrangement meant that, once the sump pan was removed, the oil pump could be taken out and serviced without splitting the crankcase – or, for that matter, removing the engine. The oil pump was a double rotor trochoid type driven from the primary shaft via the kick-starter gear. It consisted

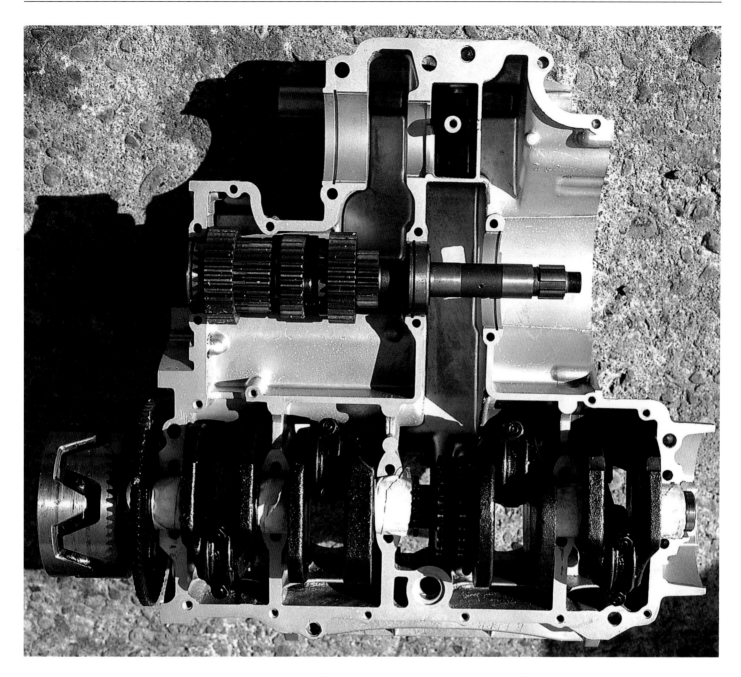

of delivery and scavenge pumps, a leak-stopper valve, installed to prevent the tank emptying its contents into the sump when the bike was stationary, with dead engine, for any considerable time, and a relief valve set to maintain constant oil pressure, dumping any excess into the sump pan. The valve was incorporated into the delivery side of the pump; standard settings were 56.9psi at 4000rpm at an oil temperature of 176°F.

The pump delivered oil through a gallery cast into the lower crankcase, and forward to the full-flow oil filter located at the front of the lower crankcase. The filter had a by-pass valve built in so that if the filter became clogged, oil, though unfiltered, would still flow through to the crankshaft. Oil went through the filter for purifying before being sent through another cast-in gallery to a main gallery cast into the upper crankcase

behind the cylinder block. This gallery was plugged at either end – on the right-hand side by an oil path cap which, with an O-ring, was screwed into the end of the gallery (the purpose was to allow an oil pressure gauge to be easily screwed in, to check pressure), and at the other end by a plug with an integral O-ring held in place by the alternator cover. About a third of the way along this gallery from the right-hand side a tapped hole held a screwed-in oil pressure switch. This operated a light in the tachometer which came on if oil pressure dropped below 7.1psi. Two feeds were taken up the inner two rear cylinder studs, serving the camshafts and the rocker gear. Surplus oil dropped to the sump where the scavenge pump picked it up through a built-in strainer at the bottom of the pump. Oil was then returned to the tank. In addition, an oil gallery taken off

CB750 top crankcase: on view are crankshaft with rotor and starter motor gears fitted, and gearbox mainshaft.

Engine number stamp (right) from a very early CB750, with exit of engine wiring harness also in view. The number was found in this position on all models except Hondamatics. Main bearing journal letter stamping position (far right) was common to all 750 sohc models.

Main oil gallery plug on early 750. Note rough finish of 'sand-cast' crankcase, which can be compared with a similar illustration of a 'die-cast' type on page 108.

the scavenge side fed oil across the engine to the counter shaft bearing end plate. This lubricated the ends of the main shaft and counter shaft. A tray, supplied by splash from the rotating gears, fed oil into the end of the final drive shaft; after going through a felt, the oil lubricated the rear chain by centrifugal force. One of the great benefits of these galleries was that when the crankcase was dismantled for servicing they could be easily cleaned and blown out.

On the front left-hand side of the engine the alternator cover housed the field coil, which was secured by three screws and copper washers, and the alternator stator, held by four screws. Wiring for these exited at the rear of the cover through a rubber grommet – a point of oil leakage unless plugged by silicon or similar sealer, especially on an older bike where the rubber has hardened.

These wires, of which there were five (three from the stator and two to the field coil), then joined up with two more, one from the oil pressure switch and one from the neutral switch, and joined into the engine wiring harness which exited through a cut-out in the sprocket cover. The harness was clipped to the crankcase safely clear of the chain.

On the front of the engine went the oil filter housing, with the filter case held on by a bolt. As previously mentioned, a check valve was incorporated, with an O-ring for sealing. The bolt held the filter setting spring, washer and element. The washer is almost always missing as it sticks to the oil filter and gets thrown away with the element. Check your filter: if the washer is missing, there could be a loss of oil pressure. The case was changed from a round type, at engine number 1004148, to a finned type. The reason? The oil filter case could crack around the filter bolt boss as owners over-tightened the filter bolt. Accordingly, the bolt was changed at the same engine number, 1004148, for one with a smaller, 12mm socket size, head. It was imperative to use a torque wrench to tighten to 22-24lb ft, or the head would round off. This is a point of some amusement to those in the trade, for the warnings to use a torque wrench never seemed to deter the 'tighter the better' merchants, as evidenced by the number of machines running around with a socket welded to the butchered bolt.

On the front right-hand side of the engine were the ignition advancer and contact points assembly. The advancer was of centrifugal type, pegged to the end of the crankshaft. Outboard of this was the points plate holding two sets of points and condensers and attached to the crankcase with three 5mm screws. Stamped into the advancer face were markings for top dead centre of numbers 1 and 4 cylinders and 2 and 3 cylinders, plus the F marks for ignition timing and two slash marks, for the advance to be checked. A dummy nut in the points cam end of the advancer, held by a 6mm nut, facilitated engine turning. The points were covered by a chromed steel cover with 'HONDA' stamped into it and secured by two countersunk screws. The wiring was fed through a rubber grommet in the crankcase at about 8 o'clock and clipped up just in front of where the clutch cable entered the clutch housing, with the lead running behind the oil feed and return pipes and then up the rear of the crankcase, to join the main wiring harness.

This effectively finishes my description of the bottom end of the engine.

The cylinder block was a one-piece alloy assembly with iron liners extending down into the crankcase to support the piston skirts. It was located to the crankcase by two knock pins. Sixteen through studs retained the cylinder and cylinder head to the crankcase. The pistons were of cast aluminium, with flat tops, giving a compression ratio of 9:1; there were small cutouts for the valves and an arrow pointing to the exhaust port indicating correct fitting. Pistons were available in four over-sizes – 0.25mm, 0.50mm, 0.75mm and 1.00mm – to facilitate reboring, and were attached to the con rods by conventional gudgeon pins located by two circlips. The pistons had a normal three-ring set-up comprising two top rings and a one-piece oil control ring (later changed to a three-piece type). Located in the cylinder was the cam tensioner, held to the rear of the cylinder by three bolts, easily removed from the outside. The tensioner consisted of a push bar which, via a cut-out, was capable of being locked by an external bolt and lock nut. This push bar bore on the tensioner assembly, which fitted to the top of the crankcase by means of a pin held by two rubbers. The tensioner had two wheels built into it, one removable, through which went the cam chain; the tensioner was firmly clamped to the crankcase by the cylinder assembly. At the front of the cylinder was a guide held by pins, one removable, which bore on the cam chain.

The cylinder head, like the block, was a one-piece alloy casting, with hemispherical combustion chambers. It was held to the cylinder block by two knock pins, although these were not interchangeable with the cylinder pins. It had two valves per cylinder working in pressed-in guides. Steel valve spring seats received twin springs topped by a keeper and a pair of split collets. The valves were worked by a single overhead camshaft rotated by a detachable sprocket held by two special bolts; the shaft ran in its own separate pair of cam carriers bolted to the cylinder head top surface. This system gave some trouble on the

early models as the 6mm bolts were not really up to the job, and certainly not in a tuned engine with radical camshaft. There were two split bearings each, and extensions which carried the rocker arms and shafts. The carriers supported two shafts each and were longer for the inlets to match up with the valve spacing. Cylinder block and cylinder head were bolted down by through studs, as mentioned previously, having flange nuts and thick washers. The camshaft was lubricated under pressure, oil running up the two innermost rear cylinder studs from the main oil gallery at the top of the crankcase and being distributed through two very small drillings in the cylinder head which mated with holes in the cam carriers supplying the rocker arms and shafts. The joint was sealed by two small O-rings – no room for dirty oil here! Four additional 6mm bolts accessed through circular rubbers gave extra sealing between the cylinders, assisted by a bolt at the extreme centre rear of the cylinder head.

The cylinder head was crowned by an extremely handsome cam box which also carried the rev counter drive, turned by worm gear from the right-hand end of the camshaft. The cam box had eight separate circular caps through which the valve clearances could be set by screw and lock nut – no fancy time-consuming shimming here! Built into the cam box was the breather system, with a pipe exiting the rear of the cam box and opening to atmosphere at the right-hand rear of the engine, via a detachable cover of triangular shape . On the rear of the cylinder head were four rubber pipes to which the carburettors were attached. The spark plugs were 12mm NGK D8ES accessed via deep tunnels cast in the cylinder head. The middle two plugs are very difficult to get to without the correct tool, and as a result stripped threads in the cylinder head are not uncommon – and repair is almost impossible with the engine in the frame. On the exhaust side, four chromed steel joints, which were held to the cylinder head by two countersunk screws, and sealed by copper rings, carried the exhaust pipes. The engine was put into the frame from the right-hand side and held in place by three long bolts, the rearmost of which also supported the rider's footrests. There were also two detachable plates at front and rear and a casting on the left front of the frame through which there was also an attaching bolt.

Carburettors & air cleaner

The carburettors were of Keihin manufacture – and, of course, there were four of them. Carburation was one of the aspects of the CB750 that had motorcyclists of the day aghast and mechanics hoping for early retirement. Truthfully, the carbs

Bare cylinder head and camshaft (from a K6), with rev counter worm drive and cam sprocket on the latter. Note valve spring spacing and final-type camshaft oiling jets.

Early CB750 carburettors and air cleaner box, with segments on throttle stop screw and blanking screw for vacuum take-off.

were not as complex as the motorcyclist believed or as difficult to set up as the mechanic feared. In fact it was all just like working on CB72/77 twins, two at a time. All four carburettors were fitted to a plate, so that if they were removed they remained together as a set. They were ordinary slide-type carburettors of 28mm venturi, with 120 main jets, 2.5 slide cutaways and 40 slow-running jets. The main difference from having four entirely separate carburettors was in the plate to which they were attached, and the choke mechanism, operated from the left-hand carburettor by a series of links to each carburettor.

The carburettors were connected to the engine by four short rubber manifolds, as noted earlier, which were directed to meet the angled ports of the cylinder head. The ports were angled to keep the carburettors clear of the rider's knees (at cost of a slight loss in efficiency). The throttles were operated from the twistgrip by a four-into-one throttle cable, with the junction box under the fuel tank. The very first bikes were delivered with very lightweight throttle cables, but these were replaced early in the production run as there was a possibility of their snapping. An adjuster was built in at the twistgrip end, for free play, and each carburettor had an adjuster on top for individual adjustment.

Four screws were built into the manifold side

Early CB750 choke arm and linkage. Warm-up was a matter of a minute or so.

Very early carburettors (facing page), removed for inspection and seen from both sides – these were soon to be changed for the K1 model. Small adjusters on top of the carbs were changed under warranty for larger, more reliable adjusters.

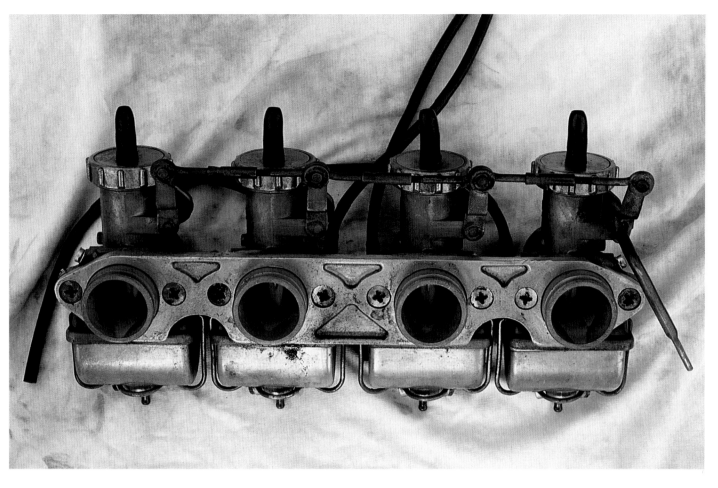

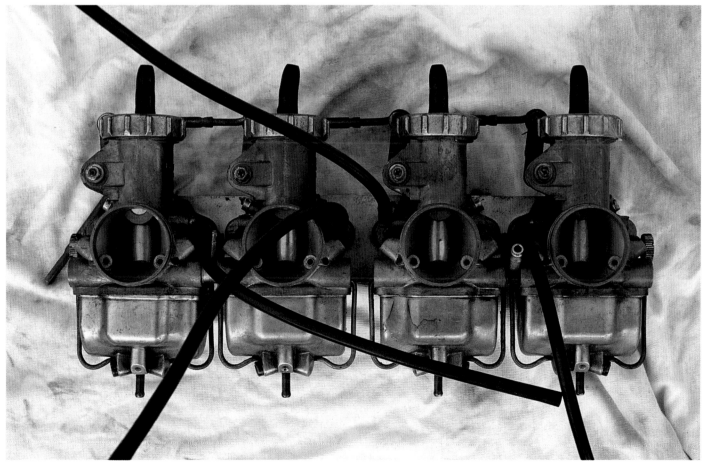

of the carburettors into which adaptors could be fitted which connected to a set of vacuum gauges, to aid carburettor balancing. This made life easy for the mechanic, in that all that was needed for balancing were a pair of spanners and a set of vacuum gauges – available from Honda at astronomical cost, though after-market versions were considerably cheaper and just as good. There was a sort of built-in 'cruise control', in that you could adjust a screw and lock nut on the twistgrip housing to enable the grip to be set in one position – very convenient for straight roads in places like Texas and Arizona. The finish of the carburettors was bare zinc alloy. The float bowls were slightly polished and had screws built in which enabled the chambers to be drained of fuel; the bowls were attached to the bodies by a spring clip, for easy removal.

The air cleaner was painted in body colour and fitted at the rear of the carburettors. It came in two portions, the bottom section being removable to allow one to inspect, clean or replace the paper element housed there. It was held to the top case by two wing nuts. The air cleaner case was rigidly mounted to the frame by two brackets and as a result suffered from cracking; even several modifications failed to cure this annoying and expensive trait and so the case was completely redesigned for the K1 model. The air cleaner was connected to the carburettors by four rubber

Early CB750 silencers: these type 300s are loud – but thrilling. Satin-chrome heat shield on upper silencer protects passenger's legs and feet.

Early number 4 exhaust, original and extremely rare: there is neither a cut-out for the brake pedal nor an HM 300 stamp.

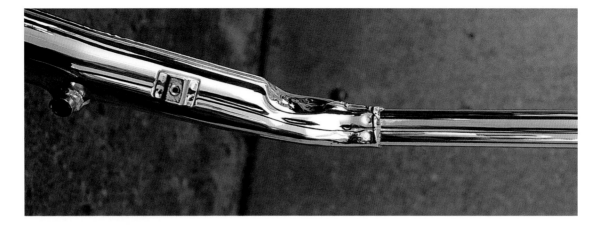

The normal indent required for brake pedal clearance (right), and a replacement early number 1 silencer (far right) with HM 300 stamp.

Finned exhaust clamp (right) on an early bike seems almost redundant in Japanese engineering. Silencer connecting band (far right) was one of the few CB750 parts that remained unchanged from the first to the last of the four-silencer series.

tubes. This assembly is one of the most difficult parts to source during a restoration, and also extremely expensive. Luckily, remanufacture is now being undertaken.

Exhaust system

The exhaust system comprised four separate pipes, each of which was in one piece with individual silencers/mufflers welded to the downpipes. The downpipes were double-skinned for some of their length to stop 'blueing' and were fitted to the cylinder head joints by finned split collars. The top silencer on each side had a heat shield screwed to it to save a pillion passenger's feet from direct burning contact. This was satin-chrome on the early models. The two silencers on each side were inter-connected at the extreme rear by a short rubber tube held by a black anodised clamp. Removable baffles fitted into the rear of the silencers and were easy to clean until Honda started to weld the nuts in place to stop people removing the baffles completely. The exhaust note is particularly strident with these removed! Baffles and connecting tubes fitted rather poorly and leaked frequently. A rubber buffer for the side stand and a corresponding one for the centre stand were fitted to number 2 exhaust. The top two exhausts had tubes welded through them for the pillion footrest bolts. Otherwise, apart from the fact that the pipes could rust at an alarming rate from the inside, if the machine was used for frequent short runs, the exhaust system was a visual tour de force, being fully chrome-plated, and one of the outstanding features of the machine.

Transmission

At the first stage of transmission was the primary drive sprocket and integral shock absorber, which was fitted to the mainshaft and driven by the primary chainset; underneath was the primary chain tensioner. This consisted of a spring-loaded arm at the end of which was a rubber roller pressing against the chains, and held in the lower crankcase by a peg and 6×16mm bolt. The sprocket was integral with a short, splined shaft, which was hollow to accommodate the mainshaft. Inside were two needle roller bearings for the mainshaft. The shaft ran through a 6008 ball bearing to the clutch drum, to which it was splined. This bearing was a weak point in tuned engines and hard-ridden standard machines. It was changed at engine number CB750E-1005307 to a type located by a set ring.

The mainshaft was splined to the clutch centre and ran on ball bearings at either end. Mainshaft and primary drive shaft bearings were located in the crankcase by set rings. To the mainshaft were fitted five gears meshing with the five gears on the countershaft positioned behind and below the mainshaft. The countershaft ran on ball bearings located on the right-hand side by a housing in the crankcase and at the left-hand side by a removable bearing holder which was attached to the lower crankcase by four 6×20mm flat-head screws, centre punched at the factory to stop them coming loose. The bearing holder was used to feed oil from the lower main oil gallery to the ends of the main and counter shafts. The gears were selected by a trio of selector forks controlled by a barrel cam fitted into the lower crankcase. The cam had an indent which lined up with a neutral switch fitted into the lower crankcase and was accessible from the outside of the engine after removal of the number 2 cylinder exhaust pipe.

The final sprocket was driven not by the counter or main shaft, but by its own shaft, via a 47-tooth gear on the right-hand end of the

counter shaft which meshed with a 56-tooth gear. The shaft was located, in its own separate housing in the crankcase, by two roller bearings and set rings. The sprocket was fitted to a spline and locked in place by the usual Honda practice of offset splined plate and two 6×12mm bolts. These bolts were increased in length at engine number CB750E-1003527 to 16mm to accommodate a change in sprocket and shaft size introduced at the same engine number. There were many changes to the final drive shaft, and these will be dealt with in the model-by-model chapters, starting on page 62.

As well as an electric starter, there was a folding kick-starter, located at the extreme rear right-hand side of the engine. It was fitted to a shaft carrying a large gear and pawl and ratchet mechanism with a return spring. The large gear meshed with a gear integral with the back of the clutch drum, giving primary kick-starting. The

Exhaust sticker on early CB750 (top) warns against modifications to the standard system. A thousand four-into-one exhaust manufacturers took no notice of it! Riveted plate on early type 300 replacement pipes (above), seen 'upside-down' so it can be read easily, informed US and Canadian authorities that the silencers should have been fitted only to pre-1983 models...

Top engine case (from a K6) with crankshaft, main shaft, clutch and final drive shaft assembly in position.

shaft was prevented from moving by a roll pin, which was tapped in after assembly.

The straightforward multi-plate clutch went through many changes during the lifetime of the sohc series, but these changes were for ease of use and quietness rather than because there was anything fundamentally wrong with it (although the extra power of tuned engines could soon demolish the clutch plates). It used a steel outer, drilled for lightness, and a pressure plate of aluminium. There were six friction plates and six steel plates, with an outer band that prevented the clutch ears from spreading, and calling for two special outer friction and steel plates. The outer steel plate was held firmly to the clutch centre by a wire ring, and the centre was secured to the end of the main shaft by a Belville washer, a tab washer and a nut which needed a special peg spanner. On to four prongs cast into the pressure plate went four springs, held captive by a conventional lifter plate and four bolts. A 6003 bearing in the centre was used to house the clutch lifter. The housing was closed off by a cast aluminium cover held by nine screws, later changed to 10. In the centre, an oil seal surrounded the clutch release shaft. This bore on a steel ramp via three ball bearings set into the rear of the cover. A release arm was attached to this shaft by an 8mm nut and washer, and a peg cast into the cover held a short return spring.

Adjustment of the clutch was facilitated by a threaded shaft with O-ring which went through the centre of the release shaft and was locked by the 8mm nut used to retain the release arm. An oil seal was provided for the kick-starter shaft. A chromed steel cover retained by three countersunk screws hid all the release mechanism.

At the top rear of the engine was a breather pipe running to the oil tank. Further round, on the left rear of the engine, were two covers. The front one hid the gear-change mechanism and butted up to the alternator cover, for clean looks. Under this cover, the components were laid out straightforwardly – though appearing rather daunting at first sight – with all the levers and springs required for the positive-stop change mechanism. This took the form of a gear-shift spindle; to the end of this, protruding from the rear of the cover via an oil seal, the gear pedal was attached. The other end had an arm with claws which pulled or pushed pins on the end of the selector drum. The arm was spring-loaded either way from a peg bolted into the crankcase. Another shaft bolted into the crankcase carried the shift drum stopper arm, and the neutral stopper, and another bolt carried the positive stopper. Rearward of this cover was a sprocket cover bolted at two points to the rear of the crankcase.

CB750 clutch cover: seldom any reason to remove it…

Early type of gear pedal (far left) was a curved pressing, for transmission case clearance. Early kick-starter rubber (left) was a 'thin' type – it did not have to be very durable as the kick-starter was hardly ever used.

Cycle Parts

Frame

The frame was of double cradle type with a triple downtube head pipe section of steel construction which was stronger than people believed. The large under-tank tubing was of 1.25in diameter and the remainder of either 1in or 1.13in diameter. Even a 750 which has been crashed more than once rarely suffers a bent frame and, if it does, repair is usually a straightforward job. However, I have known some frames, usually hit very hard from the front, that have had to be scrapped because the damage interfered with the joint just under the headstock. All frames, for all models, were painted black, rather poorly.

The engine could be slid in from the right and was held by three long bolts, two plates and a short bolt on the left, at the front. The rider's footrests were attached to the lower rear engine bolt and had a fold-up facility for when they touched the road in cornering, which could be done fairly easily. The pillion footrests were attached to the triangulated section at the rear of the frame between the two silencers; these were (completely) foldable when not in use.

Steering lock of early 750 – note rough finish to bottom yoke.

Early steering damper bracketry pictured here was never used on a production bike and was deleted from frame manufacture very early in the CB750's history.

Early mudguard has plain, unrolled ends. Could the front edge be dangerous in a smash? *You bet it could!* Twin stays were of half-round section.

Early CB750 grab handle. Large number 8 type bolts were unique to early models. Headstock sticker (below) on early

American CB750: this one is a reprint and does not have a date stamp on it in the bottom right-hand corner, as it should.

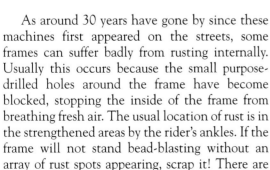

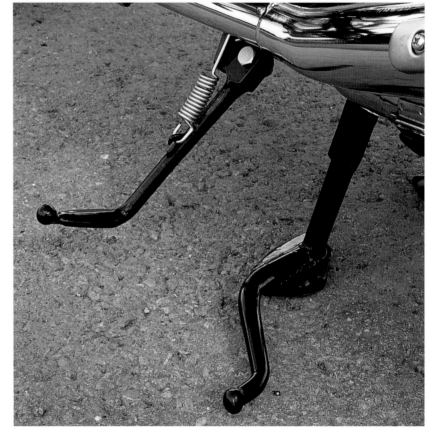

As around 30 years have gone by since these machines first appeared on the streets, some frames can suffer badly from rusting internally. Usually this occurs because the small purpose-drilled holes around the frame have become blocked, stopping the inside of the frame from breathing fresh air. The usual location of rust is in the strengthened areas by the rider's ankles. If the frame will not stand bead-blasting without an array of rust spots appearing, scrap it! There are

plenty of good ones out there. I must say, however, that rusting out is the exception to the rule, as the frame is normally a solid unit.

Stands

The machine was fitted with both centre and side stands of conventional pattern. The side stand was operated from the left-hand side and bolted to a lug welded to the frame. The centre stand was

(Top) Centre stand as fitted on early models. Early CB750 has no strengthening bar on the centre stand (above) nor any side stand additions.

Front forks were of conventional type (above). Note lack of a speedo cable guide. Early small oil seal fork case (above right). New bikes were delivered with a lacquered polished satin finish to the lower forks which soon deteriorated. British tax disc is a reminder that first Ks qualify for tax exemption!

also operated from the left-hand side, by a tang integral with the stand, and fitted to the frame by a shaft which went through two split lugs, with locking by two bolts and extra security by split pin through the shaft. An unusual thing about the centre stand was the spring mounting, which used a curved plate to connect the spring to the frame – done to provide clearance for the previously mentioned shaft. The centre stand was modified early on with an extra strengthening rod between the tang and the left-hand leg of the stand, to avoid possible weakening of the tang. Both side and centre stands were painted black, with the springs, bolts and centre stand spring plate and shaft in a zinc-plated finish. A chrome-plated grab handle was attached to the top-left shocker bolt to use when heaving the bike on to the centre stand.

Swinging arm

Colloquially – always! – known as a swinging arm but more sensibly described as a pivoted fork, this part of the 750's anatomy was fitted to the frame in conventional manner via a through bolt, collar and two phenolic plastic bushes. The pivot was lubricated by two grease nipples, one in each end of the bolt. Problems were to be found here from lack of, or improper, lubrication. The only sure way to avoid trouble was to remove the fork – no, might as well give up and call it the swinging arm! – and clean and lubricate liberally. But who did this? Very few. The arm was made from two pressings, for strength, with a tube welded in for the pivot and two cast lugs welded to the rear for the axle, bottom shocker mount and chain adjusters.

Three-quarter frontal shot of early CB750 Honda highlights graceful fuel tank styling.

A plastic chainguard was bolted to the left-hand side of the swinging arm. This was lengthened at frame CB750 1021879 to stop the pillion passenger getting sprayed with chain lube. Later it was made of metal, to prevent splitting. The early plastic chainguards are very rare, and when you do find them they are often useless on account of the cracks and scratches for which they were notorious. The pivot bushes were changed to a sturdier type later on, hopefully the better to endure the arduous conditions they were exposed to. And indeed these are better at putting up with lack of

Fuel tap has three positions. Above it is the plain aluminium strip running around the bottom of the tank.

Rear shock absorber on early 750. Intact chain guard, as seen here, is rare.

Early de Carbon-type shock absorber made by Showa – an under-rated unit.

grease, but only just. The best way to keep on top of the matter with these bushes is to remove the swinging arm completely when the time comes to change the rear tyre. The arm was painted in the same black as the frame and had a sticker on non-UK models on the right-hand arm telling the customer not to fiddle with the exhaust system. Not many took the blindest bit of notice!

Suspension

There were no real surprises here. Although it can be argued that it was 15 years before suspension caught up with the engine power of Japanese motorcycles, I personally think this is unfair, for the forks were perfectly adequate for most riders. As with the Gold Wing later, there were riders who weighed 20 stone and wives, but not girl-friends, of course, who weighed 18 stone who complained that the suspension was too soft. Not surprising, really. Then there'd be the rider who was 8 stone wet through, and complained that it was too hard; also not surprising. It is one thing having three days and just one rider to tune the suspension to suit (as in racing); but to launch a machine to be bought by thousands, a compromise has to be the only answer, even in the '90s.

The front forks were of a conventional type. Each bottom case held a fork pipe. There were two bushes per fork leg. The top one was stationary, held by the oil seal and its circlip, and the fork tube slid up and down through it. The lower one was attached by clips to the fork tube. Damping effect was governed by holes drilled in the fork tubes (one hole per leg to chassis number CB750 1039119, two holes per leg thereafter) which were covered and uncovered by a damper valve held by circlips. An oil seal was retained by circlip in the top of the fork bottom case and, very sensibly, a pair of gaiters was provided for additional protection from dirt. The lower case had a split clamp at the bottom to enable the front axle to be secured. This clamp was special in that it had to be fitted one way round only, an arrow (added later) denoting this, and the front nut tightened first, as the clamp was split unevenly; then, when the rear nut was tightened, a small gap remained. Coil springs were fitted down the middle of the fork tubes. The forks were topped off by two body-colour head-lamp brackets, which also held the turn indicator stalks; the brackets helped to provide protection from dirt for the top of the forks. The brackets were rubber-mounted top and bottom, and a small chrome ring covered the top of the gaiters, for a clean finish. The damper oil, originally of SAE 10/30 viscosity and 220-230cc capacity per leg, could be drained by removing a 6mm bolt at the bottom of the forks, and refilled after removing a 19mm headed bolt at the fork top which held the

Early CB750 filler cap permitted one-handed removal, which was deemed dangerous.

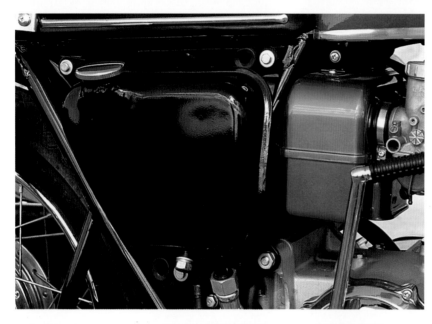

Early CB750's stylised side cover removed, reveals oil tank. Detail view (below right) shows one of the rubber pads on which the removable panel seats.

A minor advantage of the dry-sump system for the rider is that there is no danger of burned fingers when checking oil level. Dipstick, integral with cap, has clear markings for maximum and minimum level. The sohc 750 was not an oil burner.

Early 750 oil tank sticker: Honda used to advise oil and filter changing at 2000 miles.

Side panel badge as fitted to early 750s, and now obsolete – it was soon dropped for a less elegant design, for the K2.

Early CB750 front hub, featuring speedo drive cover without bulge.

fork spring in place. The forks were attached to the frame via cast iron bottom and cast alloy top yokes, with separate ball races. A steering lock was incorporated in the bottom yoke, an unusual and extremely awkward-to-get-at position, as well as an attachment for the brake line joint.

The rear suspension utilised radical de Carbon gas-filled units which, however, looked entirely conventional. They were fully chrome-plated. The only adjustment was for spring pre-load, done by ramped cam. The shock absorber consisted of a sealed damper unit with rod which was mounted upside-down, with the rod attached to a chromed bottom tube by a nut. In assembly, the ramped cam was slid over the bottom tube, then the spring, then a chromed cover. The chromed cover was then compressed and a pair of polished alloy spring seats slipped in over a ring fitted to a groove in the damper body. They were attached to the frame at the top and the swinging arm at the bottom by rubber mounts built into the shock absorbers. These units could be completely stripped for maintenance, which is a boon for the restorer, allowing all parts to be replated and polished easily; alternatively, complete damper units are still available. The units were built by Showa under licence from de Carbon.

Fuel & oil tanks

The fuel tank was of appealing shape and held 5 gallons, according to the owner's manual. It had a central cap that was styled to look like a racing-type device. Early model caps could be opened by one hand, in one easy movement. This feature was soon changed to two-handed operation, for safety reasons. The fuel tap, with an internal filter, was fitted on the right-hand side and had three positions: on, off and reserve. It fed two pipes, one feeding carburettors 1 and 2, the other carburettors 3 and 4. A bowl was removable at the tap's bottom to clear out any sediment, and to clean the filter situated therein.

The tank was fitted to the frame by two rubbers at its nose and by a rubber to which it could be clipped at the rear. Two stripes went down the tank from front to rear in gold and black. A 'HONDA' die-cast badge was fitted either side. Two strips sealed the seam at the bottom of the tank. These early strips were of plain chromed plastic and were always very difficult to obtain, having been superseded early on by the black-strip type. An easy way around this, for a restorer, can be found in use of the seams of an old Mini.

The oil tank was under the right-hand side cover. It was painted black on all models and bolted via rubber mounts at three points to the frame. A removable bolt, interchangeable with the one in the sump, was provided for draining the

Super Speed front tyre (top) for an early CB750 – 'F2' on side wall has no Honda relevance. Early 750s were shod with Japanese Dunlops or Bridgestones (above) displaying these tread patterns. Rounded-shoulder rear DID steel wheel rim (left) on early CB750.

Early front disc brake caliper details. Silver finish and unique mudguard top mounting are found on early caliper bracket (above). Early method of inner pad 'B' fitting and Allen bolts holding caliper halves together (below).

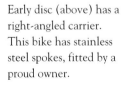

Early disc (above) has a right-angled carrier. This bike has stainless steel spokes, fitted by a proud owner.

oil. On top at the rear was to be found a dipstick for easy oil level checking – not that the CB750 ever had a reputation for oil usage. The side cover was attached to the oil tank by rubber mounts and painted in the same colour as the fuel tank, headlamp brackets, headlamp shell, air cleaner housing and left-hand side cover. A sticker was next to the dipstick, giving oil capacity information. This sticker is now obsolete but available through the restoration grapevine. Both right- and left-hand side panels carried a badge that consisted of a Honda wing with 'hm' underneath and '750' above. These badges are now officially unavailable, and consequently much sought-after.

Colours of the painted parts were Candy Blue/ Green (the most common), Candy Ruby Red and Candy Gold (which I have never seen).

Wheels & Tyres

The wheels had 40 spokes, the steel rims being of DID manufacture, with a small 'DID' logo pressed into them. The early bikes had a rear rim with a noticeable roundness to the sides. Front and rear hubs were of cast aluminium, the front one housing two 6302 bearings, the rear two of 6304 size. For the front one, on the left-hand side, an oil seal fitted into an aluminium bearing retainer which threaded into the hub, a special tool being required to fit or remove it. On the right-hand side was an O-ring, speedo drive plate and a chromed steel cover. The axle went in from the right-hand side, holding the speedo drive in place, then continued through the hub via a left-hand spacer and into the axle nut. The rear wheel was of similar design but had a larger hub, to accommodate the rear brake drum. It also had two bearings, both of the larger 6304 type, with the left-hand bearing held in place by a larger bearing retainer. A sprocket carrier was fitted to the rear wheel by four vane-pattern rubbers in the usual manner and a sprocket of 45 teeth bolted to it. This carrier had a 6305 bearing supporting it and was also fitted to the hub by a bearing retainer. The rear sprocket was held by four 12mm nuts, with two tongued washers per nut.

Either Bridgestone or Dunlop supplied the tyres, which came in sizes of 3.50S×19in front and 4.00S×18in rear, both of four-ply rating. Pattern and size remained almost the same through to the tyres used on the K5, although there were minor updates from the K1 on.

Brakes

The braking system was one of the revolutionary features of the CB750. By using a front disc brake, Honda overcame the problem of stopping a heavy motorcycle reliably and consistently. It consisted of a disc of stainless steel, of 11.7in diameter, riveted to an aluminium carrier bolted to the left side of the front hub. A swinging caliper was attached to the left-hand fork bottom case. The caliper was a two-piece type held together by two Allen bolts. The inner half carried one brake pad by a peg and split pin, the outer half the sliding outer pad and the piston and its seal. Sandwiched between the two caliper halves was the arm on which the caliper swung to take up pad wear; this arm was attached to a bracket bolted to the fork bottom. Free play was adjusted by a screw and lock nut, which was spring-loaded, the screw going through the caliper arm and a special boss cast into the fork bottom case. The caliper was activated from the master cylinder mounted via a two-piece clamp to the right-hand handlebar, fluid being piped by two rubber hoses through a junction box which held the front stop switch. This was a fine brake for its time and even now is perfectly adequate for use on modern roads; however, a twin disc kit could be fitted, supplied by Pops Yoshimura.

The rear brake was a conventional 7in single-leading shoe drum brake, with the drum being part of the rear hub. A steel liner was sunk into the hub to take the drum and the shoes were attached to the brake plate and operated by a chromed arm.

Early CB750 brake pipe junction and hardware. Chrome-finish banjo bolt was featured on only a few models, apparently chosen at random.

The brake plate was prevented from turning by a stamped-out steel torque arm bolted to the swinging arm. The brake was operated by rod from the right-hand pedal, which was chrome-plated. A small rear brake light switch, on its own bracket, bolted to the frame, was actuated by a short spring attached to the pedal. Adjustment was by a 14mm headed nut threaded to the rear of the brake rod. All, as you can judge, entirely normal practice – especially when compared with the revolutionary front brake.

Seat

The stylish dual seat had a raised flip at the rear which distinguished it from all other seats used on Hondas. It was hinged, and access was by spring-loaded catch on the left-hand side of the machine, near the top of the rear shock absorber, which one pulled to the right. With the seat raised, battery and tool kit could be reached, as well as the rear light and indicator feeder wires. The seat had a strap between the front and rear sections for the pillion passenger to hold and a stainless trim around the bottom. The cover was quilted and the

CB750 master cylinder for the front disc brake. Note lack of brake pipe cover and chromed union bolt. Clearly seen are early-type black knob 'kill' switch and dip-switch.

CB750 rear hub brake, with number 8 bolt clamping brake arm (left).

Note how the brake shoe pins are set into the brake plate (above).

Besides clutch cover and kick-starter, this shot shows early rear brake pedal without stop and number 8 bolt holding the brake light adjuster. Also on view is one of the oil pipes of the dry sump lubrication system.

An original CB750 seat is a rare find these days, although scarcity is no reason for despair as after-market makers supply replacements of superb quality. Original seats were poorly made, splitting very quickly after the interior foam collapsed.

Seat hump with aluminium beading on early CB750.

Early seat lock on the left side was of eccentric design, consisting of a spring-loaded catch which had to be pulled to the right to release the seat.

interior foam made from many separate pieces. Although the early seats were, to my mind, the most stylish, they soon sagged and tore. An original early seat is extremely difficult to find. Luckily, the pattern seats now being made are as good as, if not better than, the originals.

Handlebars

The handlebars were of conventional pattern, with about 4in rise, and swept back for wrist comfort. There were two knurled sections, midway, where the handlebar clamps fitted, to prevent accidental rotary movement. Wiring for the right and left switchgear was routed through the bar, rather than being in the open, in the usual fashion, and this made for a notably clean and uncluttered look. Another drawback, of having the control clamps loosen, was avoided by a simple hole (in the bar) and peg (in the switchgear clamps) arrangement. Why hadn't the Brits (or the Germans or the Italians) thought of this?

As for the shape and height of the bar, the Americans liked it but European riders thought it should be lower and flatter, and quite a few went to considerable trouble (drilling, threading wiring and so on) in fitting replacement handlebars of their choice.

Handlebars of conventional pattern (facing page), with about 4in rise, fitted to an early bike; later bars are subtly different. Note early Stanley sealed beam headlight.

Electrics

Lighting & Wiring

The electrics on the CB750 were excellent, and in fact probably better than today's untestable, untraceable, over-priced systems – although I have to concede that modern electrics are very light, sophisticated and reliable. But at least you can repair the CB750's if they do go wrong.

All the lighting parts were made by Stanley. The headlight was a sealed beam type for the US, Australian and 'general export' markets, and a replaceable bulb type for the rest. This was the only part of the electrics regularly improved by owners, as the light did not put out enough power for hard riders. One of the neatest, most effective improvements was installed by Mark Wigan, whose comments on other aspects of CB750 ownership have appeared earlier in this book (see pages 10-20). I quote him again, from a brief article published in *Motorcycle Sport* in 1971.

'After spending the horrendous sum of £684 on a certain four-cylindered Japanese motorcycle, I was disgusted to find that the feeble glow from the headlamp was really not up to even the 70 limit at night. The reason for this is simple: the US model has a 50-watt sealed-beam unit, but the UK model has a 35-watt bulbed unit.

'The first step was to replace this standard unit with a Cibie Type 22 unit, which has a 45-watt bulb. This brought the beam intensity up to a better level, and gave a far better cut-off pattern as it has the Continental sharp cut-off setting rather than the vague British Dazzle and Blurr.

'The main observable difference when on headbeam was that the range of clear vision was noticeably better, but that the beam formed a pencil pattern with good penetration but little side illumination. This became an embarassment when swinging from lean to lean on a winding, narrow road.

'There are two further steps that could be taken; a sealed-beam unit from a car or a quartz-iodine vapour lamp.

'The car sealed-beam units come in 50-, 65- and 75-watt ratings, all for 12-volt systems, although 6-volt versions can be found. The main disadvantage of this choice is that no pilot bulb

light can be fitted inside.

'As I wanted to get as much light for as little wattage as possible, I plumped for a QIV unit. The twin features of QIV lamps are greater efficiency in converting electricity to light and much longer life at full luminosity. The effect of the iodine vapour is to redeposit the tungsten vaporized by the heat of the filament and stop it coating the rest of the interior of the lamp.

'The good heat transfer properties of the gas used in QIV lamps allow the use of thinner fila-

American market headlamp on early CB750. It gave good light.

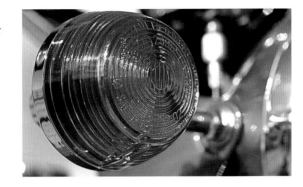

Small front indicator found on early bikes; later versions grew an inch or so in diameter.

This small early reflector was superseded, on the K2, by larger type.

Early tail lights in European…

…and American styles.

The built-in side reflector required by American regulations.

ments: this gives us a hotter and thus whiter light, and helps the lamp designer to get a much better defined focal point. The reflector can then be properly set to get all the light out to where he wants it to go.

'Several twin-filament QIV units are readily available; the Carello, the Lucas, the Wipac and the Cibie. The Lucas and the Wipac use the Phillips twin-filament bulb and are very shallow units. Versions of both are available that allow a pilot bulb to be fitted inside. At £5 10s the Lucas is probably the best buy of this class and will fit easily into any space where an ordinary unit would go.

'If, however, you feel the need of up to 110 watts of QIV/Laser reaching out in front of you, the Cibie Biode is the answer. The unit uses two single-filament QIV bulbs, and is very deep and bulky. There is no provision for a pilot lamp. As the Honda 4 has an enormous reserve of watts, thanks to its excited-field generator, the Biode can be used with the wiring set up to illuminate both dip and main beam lamps at once: thus the 110 watts.

'Physically the fitting of the Biode into the skimpy headlamp shell on the Four was quite straightforward. There is very little spare room, but it all goes together neatly if a little care is spent arranging the way that the leads inside the shell are laid out.

'Initially the unit was wired up as a simple 55/55 QIV lamp. The effect when driving was dramatic: the contrast between road and grassy verge was suddenly visible at last, even on dipped beam with strong headlmaps against one.

'The cut-off pattern was similar to the Cibie Type 22: the main differences being the rather wider spread of the dipped pattern. With the long pencil of light coming out on the roadside from this kind of beam it is possible to maintain much higher speeds than normal in comfort. The main beam was Type 22, plus a subjective 30 per cent extra range, clarity and edge lighting. In spite of this enhanced side lighting on main beam setting, it is still desirable to fill in the gaps in the light pattern near the machine.

'To do this the speedometer illumination lamp was called in to provide a suitable way to get dip bulb on 'dip' and both bulbs on 'head'.

'The effect of the plethora of lumens is exemplary: an even, untiring white light lights up the road near and far to an extent such that 70 m.p.h. is possible at night at any place where it would be during the day.

'Oncoming motorists seemed to be happier with the 110 watts of Cibie than the 35 watts of Stanley (Honda original equipment), and the contrast between dip and main did not give one that awful disoriented feeling.

'In fog, the intense dip beam is excellent and even better than the Type 22 due to the wider spread of the dipped beam.

'Unfortunately this unit costs a stiff £8 10s, but is certainly the nicest light that I have driven behind.'

Direction indicators, which were a model for anyone wanting to know how to make a good system, were chrome-bodied, circular, and attached to the front of the motorcycle by stems which doubled as headlamp bolts. Inside, the bulbs were properly rubber-mounted and the leads colour-coded. The rear indicators were mounted on separate teardrop-shaped brackets which were additionally rubber-mounted to the frame and attached by the rear mudguard bolts. The German market had a completely different type of indicator, with extended lenses easily seen from the side. These were fitted by the headlamp bolts at the front but at the rear via extended brackets welded to the rear number plate support.

The rear light was attached via the number plate bracket, in all markets; however, there were many differences to comply with local lighting regulations. The UK model had a rounded lens with a small reflector in the middle and was fitted to a black-painted number plate bracket that was unique to this market. The German model had a completely circular rear light with separate reflector situated below the number plate. The number plate bracket was a one-off, and was painted black. All other models had the same chrome number plate bracket, which was the prettiest of all, and a small squared-off light with a reflector in the middle. American, Canadian, French, Australian and 'direct sales' (factory to customer) models had reflectors in the sides as well – the one for France with an extension with separate reflector under the number plate.

The wiring harness ran from the headlamp down the left-hand top tubes of the frame, tributary wires feeding the horn which had a chrome-plated front and was mounted on the left of the frame under the headstock until frame number CB750 1003951, when it was moved to the right-hand side. Wires also led to the ignition coils mounted under the fuel tank. There were two of these, the left coil feeding numbers 1 and 4 cylinders and the right one numbers 2 and 3 cylinders. The wiring harness ran down behind the left-hand side cover under which the remainder of the electrics were situated, on their own bracket, next to the battery. Wires from the alternator, field coils, neutral switch, oil pressure switch and starter motor joined the main harness here and fed the regulator, rectifier and starter solenoid. The battery harness also plugged into the main harness here via a small fuse box housing three spare fuses.

The winkers relay was rubber-mounted to the

Early CB750 battery position and rear fuel tank cushion. Rear lighting wires are neatly routed through clips on the inner rear mudguard.

Electrics – early style. On view are the winkers relay, starter solenoid, regulator and rectifier. Note crude fuse box and unsheathed engine earth wire.

Early CB750 points cover, with grey sleeve on clutch cable adjuster.

Left-hand horn position indicates an early CB750. Also in view is redundant bracketry for a friction steering damper, which was never fitted to a production bike.

Early CB750 front brake light switch, all beautifully sealed against rain and road wash, in usual Japanese style.

Sparking plug cap on early CB750. English market models were grey plastic. Later models had metal covers (can you believe!) which provoked plenty of misfiring in wet conditions. Rough finish of 'sand-cast' head shows up well.

Early CB750 left-hand switch for direction indicators; and (far right) American bike's right-hand switch, without a sidelight position. Note black engine 'kill' knob and chromed bolts for master cylinder clamp.

cleaner box to the contact set and the rear brake stop switch wiring connectors. Altogether, a fabulous effort – simple, easy to understand, and mendable. The culprits spoiling this happy state are the two front brake light switch wires, which can come loose, and, with the frequent toing and froing of the steering, the harness, which can rub through. The rear light earth wire can sometimes give trouble with a bad connection caused by water and lack of maintenance.

Switchgear

The switchgear was mounted in two black anodised housings, one each side of the handlebars, just inboard of the grips. At the left, the indicators were operated by a knob moved to left or right. The horn was operated by a push button below. The right-hand group incorporated the 'kill' switch – a knob at the top of the housing, moved up or down from a midway 'run' position. Below was a lighting switch that operated lights on/off, on movement to the right, and the dip and main beam facility, by moving even further to the right. On models for certain markets there was a position to control a side light, between the dip and main beam. This made it rather fussy, and confusion often occurred, which resulted in a later redesign. Below (still on the right-hand side) was a push button to operate the electric starter.

The ignition switch was located under the front left-hand nose of the fuel tank on its own bracket. This was not a good position (awkward to find in the dark; burned hands – on the exhaust; susceptible to dirt; vertically placed, meaning that the keys, if part of a bunch, soon demolished the switch internals with their weight). But it took the best part of five years before the switch was re-sited to its logical place, on the fork top yoke. There were three positions. First was off, second was on, for ignition and lights, and the third position was a parking light facility which controlled only the rear light and the side light on those bikes so equipped. Many after-market brackets were sold to reposition the ignition switch nearer the clocks. In the main, however, the handlebar switches were very good and sensibly sited.

rear of the battery box. There were three types of relay: two looked the same and effectively were, differing only in wattage requirements. The American and 'direct sales' motorcycles were fitted with American-made Signa-Stat relays which were rectangular rather than circular. The wiring harness then carried on to feed the rear light and indicators. An extra arm of the wiring harness extended across the bike behind the air

Early ignition switch (far left), with a plastic plug sealing the lock mechanism. This is now a rare item. Early key (left) compared with the simpler type, without plug, introduced for the K1.

Speedometer and rev counter

These instruments were mounted, by two chromed bands, to the top yoke and were rather larger than had been seen on any motorcycle short of a Harley-Davidson. The speedometer was on the left and the rev counter on the right, constructed with a metal base and plastic sides, with a chromed cover to hide the wiring to the 'idiot' lights and panel lights. Unfortunately the plastic lenses were prone to cracking and crazing, especially if brake fluid en route to the nearby brake master cylinder was spilled on them. The faces also suffered in hot climates, blistering and going white. After-market shops used to sell vinyl covers that fitted over the clocks to stop the sun destroying them!

The faces of the instruments were in black, with light green figures, and the speedometer read in 20mph increments to 140mph. The rev counter was red-lined at 8500rpm and calibrated to 10,000rpm. Instrument lighting was superb. Because of their generous size, the clocks were

easily legible day and night. Incorporated in the speedometer and rev counter were two 'idiot' lights each, set at eight o'clock and four o'clock. Those in the speedometer were for left/right direction indicators and high beam, and the ones in the tachometer were for neutral and oil pressure.

Rider's eye view of early CB750 instrument cluster – size and clarity make the faces easily legible day and night.

Rev counter cable guide was introduced very early on, at frame number 1003951. It is seen on a K6, with this model's nasty standard-issue horn visible behind.

Special Equipment & Accessories

Tool Kit

The tool kit was to be found in a smart 'HONDA' labelled bag in its own tray under the seat. It comprised an axle wrench and bar, 45mm pin spanner, spark plug wrench, two feeler gauges of 2 and 3 thou for checking tappet clearance, a points file, 8×12mm spanner, 10×14mm spanner, 17×19mm spanner, pliers, no.2 and no.3 Phillips driver and a normal screwdriver, a lever for these, and a hand driver. While not of best drop-forged quality, these tools were more than good enough for the road-

Under-seat view of early CB750 showing tool tray position, rough finish of seat base and gloriously integrated electrics, with everything to hand.

side tasks they were designed for. Very few secondhand bikes seem to survive with the tool kit, pointing to the fact that owners probably found the tools quite useful for household tasks.

Rear-view mirrors

These were of conventional all-chromed Honda type, except for the mirror head which was secured by a 6m domed nut and washers. Loosening the nut enabled the mirror to be adjusted, and then relocked into place. The right-hand one screwed into the front brake master cylinder and the left-hand one into the clutch lever housing. The mirrors changed twice over the model run, first by having the domed nut done away with, and relying on friction. The second change was to make them larger.

After-market accessories

Accessories were a big thing in the lifetime of the CB750, with, in particular, an unbelievable number of four-into-one exhaust systems sold during the '70s.

Advertising material for the after-market makers fought to persuade you how much quicker your bike would go with their particular exhaust in place. Some of these systems were in fact atrocious and made the machine *slower*, or created a massive flat spot in engine pick-up; almost all consisted of four-into-one header pipes and a megaphone silencer, bolted to the right-hand side. Some, of course, were very good. Having one of these replacement systems meant that you could take off your expensive four-into-four original, store it, and then refit it when you sold the bike, to reap top price for 'all-original' condition. Bolting on a cheaper four-into-one also ensured that rotting out from the inside did not occur in such a widespread fashion as with a four-into-four; and further, if the bike suffered an accident, only the megaphone part needed to be replaced. The best of these pipes were produced in the USA by RC Engineering, Jardine (who supplied pipes in many different styles) and Bassani, and in Europe by Motad and Marving.

Some people felt that the front brake could do with uprating and Yoshimura used to sell a kit to double up the front discs. The twin-disc set-up was very powerful but quite expensive, and made the front wheel very heavy. Ceriani forks were also available for the CB750, although these only appealed to the seriously well-heeled, as they too were very expensive.

Cibié and Carello provided uprated halogen light units which were a great improvement over the standard headlight found on the UK-market 750s (see page 54). Low handlebars were offered

after-market, as well as some lovely fork-top clip-ons, by firms like Read-Titan and Dunstall. Glass-fibre tank and seat units were available from Read-Titan and Dunstall, and Rickman and Seeley sold complete new running gear kits comprising forks, frame, swinging arm and wheels; you then fitted your original engine, electrics and ancillaries. Kits came styled as 'café racer' or 'tourer', and a variety of different specifications within those categories was available. Bimota also produced a specially framed CB 750, but I believe only four of these saw light of day.

In America much touring was done on the CB750 and fairings became available, as well as hard luggage. These were supplied in the main by Windjammer. Later on, Rickman in the UK sold a glass-fibre 750 fairing. You could buy a plate which bolted to the handlebar clamps to resite the

Tool kit, as found on a K6, was adequate for minor on-road repairs, although quality and quantity were hardly outstanding.

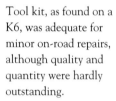

Early CB750 mirror is adjusted for angle of view after loosening domed nut.

Right-hand grip (of a late bike) with the useful Wanda-Cruise accessory, a friction device that held the throttle open. It was very popular in the USA, where it was beneficial on long freeway rides.

Ugly German and European direct sales (factory to customer) mudguard extension. Not many of these have survived!

ignition switch in a handy position, and even cigarette lighters were available. A big seller in the USA was the Wanda-Cruise, a friction device easily fitted to the throttle grip which held the throttle open on long freeway rides, easing stress on the wrist. In America too 16in rear wheels were popular, enabling owners to buy and fit a much more durable rear tyre; some even went in for car tyres, which gave fabulous mileage. Chrome-plated chain guards were available as well as engine guards, the latter a worthwhile accessory which saved the vulnerable points and alternator covers from damage in a spill. Many firms ensured their continuing existence by providing so-called King and Queen seats, so comfortable that your Honda could be ridden from dawn to dusk without so much as an ache for rider and passenger.

High-performance parts were particularly popular in Europe. I still feel that the best performance equipment was provided by RC Engineering. Normally the first performance exercise an owner did was to throw away the air cleaner, bolt on bell-mouths, jet up the carburettors and remove the baffles from the end of the silencers. When doing this did not produce enough extra urge, the next step was to have the engine bored out to 812cc. Going any further than this put you in great danger of bending a con rod, or even breaking one.

Most so-called 'performance' firms were in the business of pushing rubbish out to credulous owners. However, RC Engineering sold an engine conversion kit that they called King Cobra. This was a fantastic piece of work. It put out a guaranteed 100bhp, was more reliable than a standard engine and required no more than ordinary maintenance. You paid big money for a King Cobra conversion but most of the outlay was for strengthening engine parts that might fail with 100bhp on tap. So the connecting rods became the famous RC Golden Rods, guaranteed for life, plus a stud kit for the crankcase, and uprated bearings for the gearbox. This was all the work that was needed to be done to the bottom end of the engine to get massive increases in horsepower: 1000cc barrels and specially forged Venolia pistons, a flowed head, different camshaft, magneto ignition and strengthened rocker stands completed the package. If a wild camshaft was used with the standard ignition system, firing two cylinders at once, one having a fuel-rich charge in the inlet port, a fire was likely to occur: hence the desirability of having a magneto.

The K Series Model by Model

CB750

Release date 6 June 1969 (USA)
Frame number From CB750 1000001
Engine number From CB750E 1000001

The CB750 in its earliest form, as described component by component in the preceding four chapters, is now the most sought-after. New, they were mainly delivered to Canada and the USA. The next deliveries were to France at frame number CB750 1003495, then Germany at frame number CB750 1005084, and Australia at frame number CB750 1005130. Then came the bikes for the UK market, at frame number CB750 1010369, followed by Dutch 750s at frame number CB750 1031084. Despite Honda's official release date of 6 June 1969, I have discovered that *my* CB750 was first registered in Ottawa on 4 April 1969.

CB750 K0

Release date Unknown
Frame number CB750 1044826-1044947
Engine number CB750E 1044848-1045147

This one, as I have emphasised, was a transition model only. I do not believe any of these bikes went to America. Only 121 were made, and 36 were delivered to the UK. I do not know where the others went. The only change from the CB750 was that the carburettors became the rocker arm and linkage instruments fitted to the K1.

The carburettors remained basically the same in body. However, the plate that held the four carburettors together gained an extension to the casing, which held four rocker arms and a rod connected to a central cable plate. The cable plate carried two throttle cables, one push and one pull, so that opening and closing the throttle became a positive affair in both directions. The carburettor tops were modified to accept the rocker arms; here too were the adjusters for vacuum balance. The adjuster nuts had rubber caps to protect them. A stop screw was provided to adjust full-throttle opening, together with a common throttle-stop screw for setting engine idle speed.

MODEL DESIGNATIONS

I do not wish to enter into a massive controversy regarding the designations of the early bikes. What I am going to do is set out what is known; and how all the people I know and respect as authorities on the CB750 interpret the designations. I think all know what constitutes a 'sand-cast' bike. In fact, 'sand-cast' is the wrong term, as the crankcases of the early bikes were gravity diecast, but for the sake of peace everyone in the business knows the first 7414 engines as 'sand-casters'.

The Americans, and the rest of the world, to the best of my knowledge, call the first bikes 'K0s'. Even American Honda call them 'K0s'. They are not. They are CB750s. The K0 model was a transition bike, of which 121 were made, between the CB750 and the CB750 K1. Honda UK have confirmed this. I believe the confusion arises from the fact that the American market never had any K0 transition models, so the Americans had no need to define the bikes. I think we can all agree that the CB750 and the 121 K0s are the 'early' bikes.

Finally, no CB750 I know of has ever had a matching frame and engine number – so, reader, don't panic if you are trying to work out which bike you have.

Go by your bike's frame number. I am reliably informed that most of the first 1000 bikes were hand-assembled in California. This may explain the striking discrepancies between frame and engine numbers that occurred among the early bikes.

Engine number is highly unlikely to match frame number. This engine number plate's revised position – through 90° – shows it to be from a 750 Hondamatic.

CB750 K1

Release date 21 September 1970 (USA)
Frame number CB750 1053399
Engine number CB750E 104481

Ah! The K1. This one signalled the first real model change, and it is a great bike. There's no confusion here with the almost mythical KO and it cannot be dragged into 'Who's got the earliest model?' arguments. Though I believe the very first bikes were the most attractive, and of the purest form, some of the components that made them so were not really up to scratch.

The air box changed on the K1, and for good reason, because the early box cracked and split easily, no matter that its mountings were modified regularly. The redesign was a complete success. It would have been better finished in body colours, but the satin black, rippled design was still reasonably attractive and did its job. The carburettors shared the rocker arm and linkage modifications featured on the transition K0 model and were a definite improvement, in their ability to keep in tune. Luckily, the exhausts remained the 300 type, keeping the original lovely exhaust note and contributing to much the same on-the-road performance.

The bike's slotted side covers were redesigned to a slimmer type which did not dig into the thighs of riders with short legs. The winged 750 badge on the covers was gone, forever, replaced with a new two-piece design which lasted until the K3. The badge consisted of a small diamond with a Honda wing inside it and, above this, a device in chromed plastic edged in black proclaiming '750 FOUR'. New colours also appeared: Candy Garnet (brown), Valley Green metallic and Polynesian Blue metallic, to add to the blue, red and gold of the previous model. A smaller warning sticker for oil specifications appeared on the oil tank cover. The mirrors changed from having the 6mm domed nut at the back (slackened for adjustment) to the standard Honda friction type fitted to nearly all other models in the company's range. The old screw and lock nut type of cruise control was changed for one that could be altered on the move to compensate for varying traffic conditions.

There were very slight variations for the switchgear, the European 'direct sales' versions gaining a separate on/off switch for the headlight on the left handlebar. This was introduced originally on the early bikes for the French market, appeared on the European 'direct sales' versions of the K1, and then became virtually standard on bikes with a side light, for all markets, on the appearance of the K2. A small tip here. Don't overtighten the screw, or it will break the plastic and render the switch scrap – and a replacement

Late-type big oil seal fork case was introduced on K1.

Seen here on a K2, this revised air box, in satin black and with a ribbed pattern for strength, was a great improvement on the fragile design found on the earliest CB750s.

Facing page: bank of the 'push-pull' type carburettors introduced on the K1.

switch is not cheap! The handlebars remained the same except for European market bikes; these were flatter, and introduced on public demand. The earlier bars, although comfortable, were too high for flat-out autobahn riding. The master cylinder changed in that the brake lever span adjuster was deleted and replaced by a rubber buffer. I don't know why – but hazard a guess that the adjustable one was frequently poorly adjusted, meaning that free play was removed and a potential crash situation was possible. So the change was one of the first safety measures, perhaps?

A slight redesign of the caliper casting was the only change to the front disc brake, but the front

Ignition switch changed style for the K1, but was to remain in this stupid tucked-away position until the K7.

Speedo drive cover, as revised to suit narrower hub introduced on K1: note raised section to clear speedo drive plate.

hub changed to a narrower type, with a consequent speedometer gearbox drive redesign. The front fork remained as on the last of the early bikes except that the oil seals were upped from 45mm to 48mm diameter on a change of fork case and circlip diameter. The headlamp brackets continued in the same painted style, as did the practical gaiters on the fork legs. The fuel tank changed

little except that opening the filler cap became, as indicated earlier, a two-handed affair – a good safety measure. The moulding around the bottom of the tank changed to one with a black stripe in it which seemed less prone to fading than the previous style. The tank badges moved to a gaudier design, and at frame number CB750 1103001 a sticker appeared on the tank top in front of the filler telling you to wear a helmet. The seat lost its characteristic hump and gained a safety catch hook and spring for tension; otherwise, it remained pretty much as before, hinging from the right. Speedometer and rev counter lenses went from acrylic resin to glass, to provide better resistance to brake fluid spillage. Also, the left-hand foot of the centre stand was increased by 10mm in width, for greater stability.

The rear-wheel sprocket settled at 48 teeth, up three teeth from the previous model's, and there was a redesign to the rear wheel damper units, in an effort to improve rear chain life. The redesign amounted to a slight change in damping and spring rates, with an additional seat at the top and bottom of each spring, to prevent the springs chafing. Few other changes occurred.

A CB750 K1 is an excellent buy. Most of the original models' good points, in styling and performance, had been retained, and a host of worthwhile modifications introduced in the interest of long-term reliability. Buy one, if you can find a good example – it will rarely let you down.

CB750 K2

Release date 1 March 1971 (USA)
Frame number CB750 2000001
Engine number CB750E 2000001

The K2 was a very big selling model. As far as the UK was concerned it made up the bulk of total CB750 sales. 'British' K2s, however, came off the line early in the K2 run. Many changes were introduced on the K2, effectively distancing it and subsequent models from the earlier bikes. The K2 was the first of the CB750s to be 'refined' in an easily recognisable way. Most of the changes previous to the K2, except for the side covers, were only noticeable at the time to the trained eye; and now, of course, to the modern-day restorer, looking for absolute authenticity.

First, new paint colours were offered, making for an immediately 'different' look. Let's take the machine from the front. Nothing in the front wheel had been altered since the hub and speedo drive change occurred with the K1. The front mudguard remained the same, retaining its rolled edges. But much changed at frame number CB750 2093731. The front forks went from the early bushed type to the later (and final, for the K series)

Views of an immaculate K2 – a more 'refined' CB750 that became a very big seller. This bike is fitted with Avon tyres which seem to suit well as Metzeler alternatives.

Fully chromed heat shields over silencers of later bikes were more in keeping with glittery aspect of the bikes than previous satin-finish shields. Stamping on a type 341 silencer (far right); note marking and angled pinch bolt on the rear brake pedal.

This K2, coming from Singapore, has non-European upswept handlebars.

bushless type. This was done to answer the complaint of many riders, big or small, light or heavy, that the suspension was too hard or too soft. After some factory fiddling with fork spring rates and damper hole sizes, word came through that stiction was the problem. The previous bushed forks were suffering so much stiction that the forks were locking solid in certain circumstances, and at other times just not moving quickly enough to

react to small bumps, regardless of spring or damper rates. Honda tackled the problem by removing the separate bushes of the earlier forks and using the whole fork tube effectively as one long bush, to move up and down in the fork case. At the same time, the entire damping system was changed, with a separate bottom pipe being introduced with a built-in rebound spring and more sophisticated two-way damping. Fork seals were

A magnificent sight: the K2 engine from two left-side angles (above and left). One of the biggest changes for the K2 was to the exhaust system, the view from the rear (below) clearly showing the quieter baffles of 341 silencers.

Oil tank cover had been made slimmer and badging altered to this new style for the K1; later the colour of the lower part of the two-piece badge changed from deep red to amber for the K2. Oil tank, seen on and off a bike, differed too, being more rounded and slimmer.

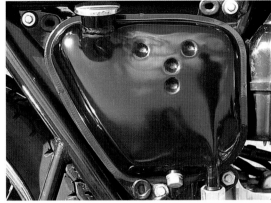

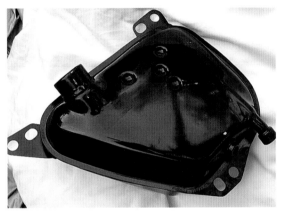

K2 fuel tank (above) with lovely gold stripe and chromed headlamp brackets. K2 front wheel assembly (left), clearly showing safer beaded-edge mudguard style and revised brake caliper. Close-ups (below) highlight the mudguard and a dab of yellow paint on the axle indicating that it was torqued down at the factory.

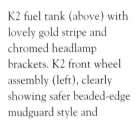

converted to a more stiction-free type, and the front mudguard rubber-mounted to the bottom fork case to avoid mudguard bracket fracture.

The de Carbon rear dampers were abandoned in favour of an oil-damped design of conventional Japanese pattern made by Showa. These dampers could not be split down as easily as the de Carbons, and as a result are more difficult to restore. But, at least, the parts are available. The new units, though internally very different, retained the all-chrome and shrouded finish of the earlier dampers.

In the USA a new, larger rear light was introduced, with reflectors at the sides and at the rear, to comply with updated EPA regulations. A winker buzzer was first heard also on the American market models at this time. It was attached to the left-hand headlamp bracket, and of course the wiring harness had to be changed accordingly. The buzzer never appeared on English market models because it was thought that the sound could be confusing, and possibly perilous, for blind people at pedestrian crossings. A grab rail for the pillion passenger was introduced on the American market K2 model, with the rear indicators bolted to it via some rather complex rubber mounts. The front indicators remained as before, as did front and rear indicators for other markets.

The headlamp shell, instead of being painted in body colour, was now black for all models, with the support brackets chrome-plated in place of the previous body colour finish. Speedometer and rev counter were changed to a type with a metal body, and on the English market model a red line appeared at 70mph on the speedo dial, to draw attention to the general, but particularly motorway, speed limit. The lenses were made of glass. Handlebar grips were changed to the infamous ribbed type, which created a whole new market for replacement grips, as they dug painfully into the hands on a run of any distance.

The chainguard changed from plastic to metal, but was still painted black. The method of fixing this to the swinging arm was modified slightly, to cure breakage – a common fault on earlier bikes. The rear sprocket was attached to its carrier by studs instead of by bolts which tended to come loose; and the anti-chain-jamming plate was increased in size. The rear brake pedal gained a positive stop, adjustable for individual taste and comfort, governing the height of the pedal. The side covers were the same as on the recently introduced K1 type, but the little diamond Honda wing badges were in amber, rather than the deep red of the K1 versions.

Probably one of the biggest changes was to the exhaust system, which now became considerably quieter than the previous 300 type. The silencers looked like the earlier ones but the baffling was considerably more restrictive. These exhausts can

be identified by '341' stamped on the upper surface of the silencers. The seat changed yet again, to a version which appeared to be made by a different company from the one that had produced the earlier seats: it had a chrome bead moulded into the circumference of the base instead of displaying the stainless strips of the previous two models. A small tray was added to the base which held the now redesigned, smaller, owner's manual. A locking seat catch was also provided, conve-

niently using the ignition key. Fuel tank badges were changed yet again, gaining some gold and a bolder appearance, and the fuel cap packing was uprated to stop leakage. The cap became the type used on the 500 four.

The colours changed completely to Briar Brown metallic, custom-flaked Sunrise Orange Candy, Candy Gold custom and Planet Blue metallic custom – the last two being the only colours available on the UK models. This was the moment when the 750's original colours were finally deleted.

Handlebar grips were changed for K2 to infamous ribbed style, which hurt your hands on longer runs. Left-hand control block shows newly introduced headlight flasher button, while throttle side block carries a big red 'kill' switch.

Revised instruments for the K2, with 8000rpm red line on rev counter and 70mph marker, reminding UK riders of the national speed limit, on the speedo. The panel of 'idiot' lights was also new. Keeping things tidy (right): rev counter cable's restricted path, as introduced on K2.

Handlebars on the European models had been changed to a lower type at the K1 model change, and the new style continued, but the higher American type were swapped for another bend pattern at the K2 stage. One of the interesting, and most easily spotted, changes came with the handlebar clamps, which, instead of being separate, were now made into a wide one-piece clamp doubling as a housing for the 'idiot' (warning) lights, with a Honda badge between. The 'idiot' lights indicated (as before) neutral, high beam, oil and turn, and their departure to the new site left the face and the internals of the instruments less cluttered. Some slight detail changes were made to the engine, but it is difficult to pinpoint the changes, for Honda followed a logical pattern of introducing modifications as and when problems arose during a model's lifetime rather than holding them back to coincide with the launch of a new K variation. Disc pads were changed at this time to try to find a way of improving wet-weather braking. Research into this area turned out to be a lengthy business, and the new pads fitted to the K2 registered only a small improvement. Today standard Honda brake pads are the best to use – but not 'old stock'. A new rev counter cable guide was fitted to the steering bottom yoke which stopped the cable escaping from its clip.

So there we have the K2, the first of the 'softened' models. Most of the glaring – not so glaring, really – faults of the earlier bikes had been dealt with, and I think it reasonable to say that the K2 was the blueprint that saw the K series through to the end.

CB750 K3

Release date 1 February 1973 (USA)
Frame number CB750 2200001
Engine number CB750E 2200001

This was the first model which was really sanitised rather than being, as previously, in the case of the

K2, merely refined. At first glance, it seemed that few changes had been made to the K2 specification, except for the gaudy new paint scheme which, apart from detail alterations, was retained right through to the K6. At this time the USA, the largest market for Honda, was being subjected to a massive 'safety' campaign throughout all commercial fields, Ralph Nader being the main protagonist. Car and motorcycle manufacturers, of course, were having to fall in line in improving their wares, and image. The K3 was a victim of all this hoo-hah; but it did help to produce an exceptionally well-sorted machine. For instance, the carburettor return spring now had a short neoprene sleeve added, to stop the two float bowl vent pipes from rubbing away. Even if this had happened, it would not have done any harm, but the modification showed the way Honda top brass were thinking about the CB750. It was almost as if they had taken a small break and sent off their most gifted engineers to concentrate on more important future matters while saying to the young apprentices, 'OK, lads, this is the best we've got. Now make it easier to use, easier to service, and make it appeal to an even wider audience'.

The air cleaner had a smaller intake hole, which helped to quieten the machine but also made it slower. With some other small changes in the assembly of the engine, coupled with the more muffling exhaust pipes taken from the K2, the engine became very quiet. To some this was perhaps a disappointment, but the whispering standard exhaust did enable those who chose not to fit a four-into-one pipe, of which there must have been 100 different manufacturers by this time, to get away with some excessive speeding. The regular population still associated speed with noise. The days in the late '90s of a Honda Blackbird whistling along at 100mph as quietly as a car had not yet arrived; but the K3 was a beginning!

Disc brake pads gained a small red line around them, making it a simple matter to peer down in front of the machine and judge when the pads needed changing. The rear-view mirrors became larger, and for the USA running lamps were added as part of the front indicator assembly. This was done by doubling up the filaments in the bulbs so that they lit as soon as the bike was running.

Handlebar switches were also changed. The high/low beam switch, instead of being situated on the right-hand handlebar block, and integrated with the on/off switch, was moved to the left-hand block. This was a particularly good idea, I thought, for I had always found the early switch awkward to use – especially, of course, in prepared-for-Britain bikes where the side-lights switch was in the middle position between high and low. On many occasions, going for the dipped beam as a car approached, I'd be plunged into

darkness, usually on a black and unfamiliar road to nowhere in particular. The headlight on/off switch, however, was still located on the right-hand block. The engine kill switch was also modified by turning it around 90 degrees so that it couldn't be accidentally knocked off, to dead engine, while you were negotiating a fastish corner. The indicator switch, on the left handlebar, where it had always been, gained a half-way position where it could be pushed gently for partial activation, which could be helpful when you were lane-changing. Letting it go returned it to the off position. To set the indicators going permanently, though, needed a good prod.

The fuse box was changed. Previously, there was only one main fuse of 15 amps, and some spares, set in a rubber moulding; now there was a proper box and the fuses were of 15 amps, 5 amps and 7 amps, for the different circuits. Another safety feature was a clutch lock-out, which meant

Disc splash guard, introduced for the K3 during the '70s scare about 'disc lag' in the wet. Also clearly on view is the caliper pivot on this K6.

that the bike could not be started in gear without pulling in the clutch lever. The forks were modified, with spring and damper rates being massaged in order to improve the ride. Disc brake pads received some attention too, to prevent squealing in use, and a splash guard was added to the rear of the left fork leg, to redirect water previously thrown up on to the ignition switch wire coupler and number 1 spark plug cap.

Separately, these small changes did not seem to add up to much, but there were a great many of them, as a look at the parts microfiche records would show. Almost all related to improved safety or ease of operation, although some appeared merely to favour ease of manufacture. Whatever, it was clear that the Honda CB750 had forever lost the rawness found in the early versions and had gone on to gain an even firmer reputation as a bike you could take straight from a dealer's showroom and ride around the world.

CB750 K4

Gear-change pattern was introduced into the external face of the transmission cover casting for the K4. Pointless? American safety legislators did not think so.

Release date 1974 (USA)
Frame number CB750 2300001
Engine number CB 750E 2300001

The main difference between the K3 and K4 was that the K4's fuel tank sported re-designed decorative stripes, with a colour change. The white

stripe became wider. The green and Candy Bacchus olive of the K3 was changed to Freedom green metallic, and the Maxim brown metallic swapped for Boss maroon metallic (your interpretation of Honda nomenclature here is as valid as mine). The transmission cover had the gear pattern cast into it, and at engine number CB750E 2304501 the carburettors' main jet was changed to a 105.

CB750 K5

Release date 1975 (USA)
Frame number CB750 2500001
Engine number CB750E 2372115

The CB750 K5 was not imported to the UK; it was mainly an American version, as was the K4. The right-hand fuel tap on the K4 was a stupid arrangement. It was necessary to take one's hand off the throttle to change to reserve (a dangerous business when flat-out on an autobahn), so it was moved to the left-hand side for the K5 and simplified in design. The friction adjuster for the twistgrip was discontinued, which made some owners disgruntled. A new side stand was fitted with a rubber casing over the operating tang, to prevent the stand digging into the tarmac if accidentally left down on getaway. The direction indicators were enlarged. The speedometer was now supplied calibrated in increments of 10mph in place of 20. Colours changed to Planet Blue metallic and Flake Apricot red. The pillion footrests now conformed to the standard Honda round pattern, and the fork seals were of uprated anti-friction type. Compound mixture for the tyres was changed, together with a slight alteration in tread pattern. And that really was that for the K5.

CB750 K6

Release date 1976
Frame number CB750 2540001
Engine number CB750E 2428762

The K6 was basically a European model which went on sale after all the K2s had been sold. It incorporated all the updated parts of the K3, K4 and K5, as well as some additions. A new plain output shaft was fitted, doing away with the rather hit and miss chain-oiler of the previous bike. An endless (ie, there was no removable spring link) rear chain was fitted, as well as a stronger F1 type swinging arm. The engine breather pipe was extended and now finished down by the right-hand pillion foot rest, held in position by its own unique bracket. The fork top yoke was modified, with smaller pinch bolts being provided to stop

CB750 K6: there were many detail changes from early bikes, but in styling broadly little difference. Why change a good thing?

Pillion footrest, seen on a K6, could be folded back when not in use. Late model kick-starter rubber was thicker than before – and helpfully identified…

With its full array of pipes and silencers, K6 was widely thought a better looker than contemporary F1.

Rubber mounting for front mudguard brace (right). Extended breather pipe on K6 directs oil mist away from rear tyre (far right).

Bold K6 tank striping and side panel badge, left-hand fuel tap and seat beading. This tank detailing was much more elaborate than for the first of the F series, also introduced in 1976. CB750 K6 rear sprocket (below) with anti-chain-jamming ring; modern O-ring chain has been fitted by owner.

ham-fisted owners (and mechanics) applying too much torque and cracking the yoke, and a separate instrument bracket appeared, coupled with re-designed instrument backs; the instrument faces were light green. UK bikes were delivered with the indicator buzzer connected but this was soon banned, because of some sensitivity, again, about endangering blind people. Carburettors were updated: the throttle-stop screw which operated on all four carburettors was located to a more convenient position on the right-hand side; slight jetting changes were made (making the bike rather slower!).

The clutch drum was modified, now being secured to the main shaft by a circlip rather than by nut and washer. To reduce clutch rattle, the interference fit between main shaft and clutch drum was tightened, which later sometimes made

K6 steering head with European 'Honda Motor Co' sticker (far left). Centre stand received a strengthening rod very early in the model's run (left).

Late-type air cleaner housing on a K6: small black plug on the pilot screw is there to deter tinkerers.

K6 front forks, with disc splash guard also on view.

it difficult to remove the clutch drum.

UK models retained the smaller, early-type indicators, but did gain the grab rail fitted originally to the American market K2. A new colour, Candy Antarese red, was on offer in place of Flake Apricot red. Small modifications were also made to rear suspension damping.

CB750 K7

Release date 1977
Frame number CB750 2700009
Engine number CB750E 2700001

The K7 marked the first touring model with any substantial change in appearance since the original CB750's launch. It was time, Honda decided, to get serious in playing at catching up with some formidable competitors – most notably Suzuki's GS 750 and the Kawasaki Z650. Both newcomers had collected excellent write-ups in the motorcycle press, displaying rather better all-round performance than the asthmatic CB750 K6. The way forward for Honda was to bring about real development in the split between the F and the K series of bikes (the F series was launched on the American market in 1975). The F series had been brought in by Honda to supersede the Ks but, bowing to pressure from the American touring market, the firm had to continue with the K series. It was decided to split their roles – F2 for 'performance', K7 for 'touring'.

Engine-wise, the bike gained a new cylinder head and camshaft, and the lighter cam sprocket featured on the F0. Crankcases were also from

K6 master cylinder cap and oil tank cover with later-style oil warning sticker.

the F0, as were pistons and rings, for slightly increased compression. The final drive shaft was also changed, as were some of the gearbox internals. However, the most visible change was to the carburettors; these were taken from the F2 and incorporated the so-important accelerator pump. Mixture settings had been leaned off to such an extent in previous models – to the detriment of performance – that this move to F2-type instruments was considered the only way to restore lost power, pending the emergence of the CV carburettor, appearing a year or two later on the twin-cam models. (Anyone who owned one of the old, 'lean-mixture' bikes will remember the age it took, sometimes 5-10 miles, for the engine to warm up and run smoothly, without use of the choke.) Another benefit of the 'F2' carburettors was that the slide mechanism was hidden under caps, which kept out the worst of the weather.

As for the chassis, other cycle parts and cosmetics, an enormous number of changes was evident; the engineers had components from the newly released GL 1000, the F1 and the F2 to play with. The K7's improvements were largely shared with the new Automatic. For instance, fuel tanks on these bikes were identical (except that the Automatic had, additionally, a fuel gauge sender). The 'idiot' lights panel, similar to that on the little 400/4, was situated between the speedometer and tachometer rather than being part of the handlebar clamps. The headlamp assembly was taken from the Gold Wing and now, at last, the ignition

Rear lamp bracket on UK-model K6, with hefty grab rail also visible.

switch on a K series bike was nicely to hand on the fork top yoke, where it should have been all along. The choke, also, was top yoke-mounted – another major improvement in user-friendliness. The front mudguard lost its forward stay, and was in fact a double of that on the F1. A retrograde move, in my opinion, was the removal of the gaiters from the front forks, which meant that the stanchions were now exposed to moisture and grit thrown up from the road, leading to premature failure of the oil seals. The headlamp brackets were changed to a simpler type, from the F1; the indicator stems were now integral with the bracket, and a small chrome trim, with Honda logo, was added to cover the bottom yoke.

Revised K6 headlamp bracket (below left), showing altered indicator stem position and one-piece meter covers. The small-headed pinch bolt defeats over-muscular tightening. Other view (below) shows rear grab rail and indicator mounting point on K6.

Instruments and 'idiot' lights panel on the K6. Note recorded mileage, and condition.

Speedo cable guide on the K6 (right) and the later separate instrument mounting bracket (far right).

CB750 K8

Released 1978 (USA)
Frame number CB750 2800001
Engine number CB750E 3000001

The K8 was an American market bike only and showed very few changes from the preceding model. Fuel tank striping was changed to gold and red, and the '750 Four' side panel badge was modified, with a fine pinstripe added underneath, incorporating a 'K' sign. There was some alteration to the seat's foam interior and covering, with the contour being more attuned to the comfort of *two* people. The colours remained the same; although I have seen a silver-coloured version that looked factory original. An obscure market machine, perhaps?

The F Series
Model by Model

CB750 F0

Released 1975 (USA)
Frame number CB750E 1000002
Engine number CB750FE 2500004

The F0 was the first of the Super Sport line of CB750s and was developed to try to win back some of the sales lost to Kawasaki, Suzuki and Yamaha. This first F was only available in America. The most notable point about it was that the trademark four-into-four exhaust system had gone – replaced by a four-into-one. Pipes and silencer were still all-chrome, but the silencer – more properly 'muffler', I suppose, for this US special – was very different from the four previously fitted, being long and tapering. The change left the nearside of the bike rather naked, which put off quite a few potential customers.

Dealers reported back to Honda that the F

A rare orange-tanked CB750 F0 – the first of the Super Sport line, available only in the USA. Engine case guards are a worthwhile accessory.

wasn't bringing in the hoped-for sales: the people out there were clamouring for the old four mufflers layout. So, as I've described on an earlier page, Honda brought in the K7 to run alongside the so-called Super Sport F with its tuned version of the last K6 engine. It had to be an uprated engine because the emphasis on quiet running and general rider-friendliness that had marked K series development in the last few years had robbed the four of much of its earlier sharpness. The F's engine took on a new cylinder head, with sportier camshaft and higher-compression pistons. Clutch basket and plates were modified, to cope with the extra power. There were closer

gearbox ratios. All this meant that the F contrasted with the previous Ks, with their easy, relaxed performance, in coming over as – almost – rev-happy.

The headlamp gained an extra 5 watts of power for each filament. The shell was from the CB500T, black as usual and fitted, together with the front indicators, on a bracket similar to the one previously seen on the 400/4. This left the forks completely naked, for that sought-after 'racing' look. Reflectors were screwed into the end of the headlamp-retaining bolts – a new 'safety' addition. One fine improvement was resiting the ignition switch on to a newly cast fork top yoke,

F0 instrument panel, with a sensibly sited ignition switch finally introduced. Panel for 'idiot' lights is a different shape, and rev counter red line is higher than on later K Series bikes. The 'phantom black' side panel of the F0 (left) is easily cracked. Badging style was different for the F series.

Even if the F0's styling was not received very well, improved performance from a high state of tune for the single-cam engine (right) was welcome.

enabling the rider to see at last where he was poking the key in the dark. The 'idiot' lights nacelle was moved to between the rev counter and speedometer, while the handlebars were carried over from the K6.

The front disc's caliper was of the redesigned type first seen on the 350/4: it weighed less than the earlier K type, was simpler, and easier to work on. The front mudguard was carried over from the K6 – although it was soon changed to a type without the forward brace. The front forks were totally new but still worked and looked the same – if a little skinnier – as forks dating from K2 days: I say skinnier because the gaiters had disappeared, which was a pity, to be replaced by a pair of dust

covers. These in fact mainly served to rub dust and dirt up and down exposed sections of the fork tubes, wrecking them in no time – and all for the sake of 'fashion'! The front wheel remained as it had been since the K2, except for a slightly redesigned brake disc.

A rear disc brake of the same diameter (11.7in) as the front replaced the drum brake of the K models. The footrests were moved backward on special cast aluminium brackets, with the right-hand one supporting the rear brake spindle (previously pivoting in a welded tube in the frame) and the hydraulic master cylinder. The kick-starter was rejigged a little, to clear these new footrest positions. The rear wheel was spoked to

With F0 sold only in America, little-changed F1 introduced the Super Sport line to the rest of the world. Bare aspect of the drive side did not please motorcyclists beguiled by the glittering exhaust system of the K Series.

match the front and gained a new hub to accommodate the disc brake, which was also used on the Gold Wing. Some small modifications were made to the chain adjusters and the chain itself was strengthened to 530 type.

The fuel tank was completely changed, becoming longer and slimmer (at 4.8 US gallons capacity), and the filler cap was recessed under a locking lid. The tank and the faired tail piece were the only painted parts of the motorcycle, now in Flake Sunrise orange or Candy Sapphire blue. Under the tail section in plastic (all right, if you really want to know…*polypropylene*) a storage compartment housed the bike manual and, perhaps, extra tools; the official tool kit was stored on a shelf adjacent to the battery. The tank retained die-cast Honda badges on its sides and the inevitable safety warning sticker. The fuel tap

was as fitted to the K6. Side covers were finished not in body colour, as before, but in a dull grey-black that Honda said was supposed to 'slim' the bike; this particular shade was Phantom black. The right-hand side cover had to be removed to check the oil level in the newly redesigned oil tank with a new plastic dipstick. The overall result was a lot of lost and broken right-hand side covers! (Secondhand ones now are, I have to say, almost impossible to find.) The side covers had simple, '750 FOUR' badges of a new type – gone was the fancy Wing. The seat was redesigned and gained a tail piece, painted in body colours, as previously noted. Two aluminium strips carried on from the fuel tank all the way to the end of the tail piece, to give a sleek look, and the seat was now pivoted from the left-hand side, a subtle improvement to make it easier, and safer, for Americans to unlock

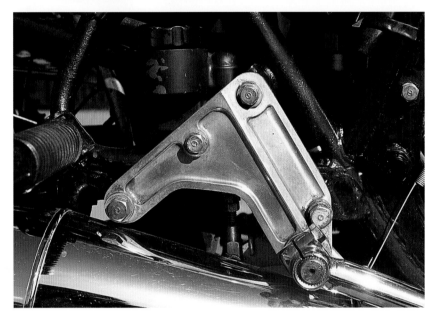

from the pavement (US motorcyclists being required, of course, to ride on the right-hand side of the road).

The four-into-one exhaust system had two separate downpipes fitting into a collector box incorporating two further, exiting downpipes. At the end of the system was a long, tapered silencer. The footrests were changed, but differed only in detail in that the rubbers were held on from underneath by two bolts, which also carried a new plate ending in a rounded 'feeler' to alert the rider that the footrests were about to hit the ground in hard cornering. (Much later, in the '90s, these are the sort of protuberances known in bikers' lingo as 'hero blobs'...) The swinging arm was strengthened, although this was not immediately obvious. Larger bushes were fitted, and a handsome chromed chainguard replaced the one-time plastic guard. The ends of the swinging arm were sealed, doing away with the axle-locking plates.

Rear shock absorbers were of usual Showa type, noticeably without the shrouds; otherwise they were as fitted to the K6. The chrome rear mudguard was deleted and replaced by a plastic guard cum tool tray retained by a new-type grab rail, which also supported the rear light bracket. The rear indicators were rubber mounted to the bracket and were of the new, larger design favoured for some other Honda models. Other changes were, first, to the frame, where a different steering head angle (28 degrees) was used to try to quicken the steering. Slight modifications were made to the frame tubes but only to accommodate other modifications such as the restyled footrest brackets and rear mudguarding. The wiring harness was changed, in that a small black plastic box was bolted to a lug welded to the left-hand front frame downtube into which went all the connectors from the right- and left-hand handlebar controls, and ignition switch, and so on.

Unfortunately, the box was quite exposed and too small to allow one to stuff the wires back in correct order once they had been removed for fault-finding! Altogether, a step backward.

So, the F0 was the first attempt to hot up the old single-overhead cammer. It wasn't received too well, because of its odd styling, and didn't recover to notch up big sales – although it could still haul people wherever they wanted to go in the usual reliable Honda way.

CB750 F1

Release date 1976
Frame number CB750F 2000003
Engine number CB750FE 2515094

The F1 was effectively an F0, and was changed very little. As the F0 was for American consumption only, it wasn't long before all other world

F1's long, tapered silencer (top left) and side stand with wear indicator on rubber (top right). Many changes were made to components, compared with the K Series. CB750 F1's right-hand, handsome aluminium footrest plate and rear brake master cylinder (above).

CB750 F1 front wheel (facing page) with redesigned caliper and modern Avon rubber.

markets had cleared their K series stocks and the F1 became available. The few changes in F0 to F1 concerned updated pistons and rings, from engine number CB750E 2551568. The front mudguard was simplified a little, losing its front stay (this had in fact happened part way through the F0 run).

The colours were changed to a choice between Sulfur yellow and Candy Antares red. All other changes were to comply with local laws. In England, for example, the original small round indicators were still used, whereas in Germany long-nosed types were the norm.

F1 rear disc brake assembly. Measuring 295mm (11.7in), the disc is very similar to that fitted in the front wheel of K Series bikes.

F1 seat: gaudy paintwork, identified rather accurately in sales brochures as Sulfur yellow, was loved – or hated.

'An awful thing to cope with' – the F1 wiring coupler box. It was too small, and once you got the wires out it was almost impossible to shove them back in.

English, French and German nationals were not the only customers to be subjected to finger-wagging lectures on correct fuel octane, helmet wear, and other matters. These instructions are seen on the tank top (above) and helmet holder (below) of a home market – Japanese – machine.

F1 swinging arm pivot area (facing page): top rear engine bracket has been redesigned and stop light switch relocated. Unshrouded F1 rear shock absorber (right): a weight-saving move or an attempt at the 'race' look?

PREVIOUS PAGES
Head-on shot of F1 shows spindly look of forks deprived of gaiters, while rear view emphasises how this machine was sadly deficient in all the exhaust orifices that so intrigued motorists overtaken by hard-ridden Ks. Mirrors are a non-standard Suzuki type.

F1 front caliper: an updated type with through bolts from the outside.

Japanese-market front master cylinder cap.

More F1 details: Japanese-market headlamp and front indicator, the latter fitted to a type of under-headlamp bracket shared with the CB400/4.

Master cylinder, right-hand switches and new moulding pattern for grip – plus the stem of an incorrect Suzuki mirror.

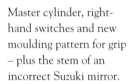

F1 from the saddle, with instruments unchanged from F0, apart from background colour. Detail shows the ignition switch position on F Series bikes, and Japanese-market speed warning light in the steering stem nut centre. Ignition key by this stage has a plastic grip.

Major changes came for the F2, Comstar wheels and black-painted engine in particular adding muscle to the looks.

CB750 F2

Release date 1977 (USA)
Frame number CB750 2100011
Engine number CB750FE 2600004

Suddenly, on the arrival of the F2, came the biggest change yet, with an engine turning out 73bhp at 9000rpm. The F2 signalled a great departure from the original CB750, with almost every part changed. Both front and rear wheels were of Honda's new Comstar pattern. These were made up of an alloy rim mated to five large steel spokes riveted to hub and rim. There was no way the wheels could be dis-assembled. The finish was

bare anodised aluminium. I have to say that Comstar wheels are a nightmare to restore; really, the only way to obtain a truly *concours* finish is to fit new wheels!

The front brake was changed to twin 275mm discs, with a new type of caliper mounted at the rear of each fork leg. These calipers were finished in black, which is about all they had in common with the earlier type. A bracket attached by two bolts to the fork had two pins fitted into it which moved laterally and allowed the single-piston caliper to take up wear in the brake pads. This was simpler than the original arrangement and also did away with the K series bikes' small swinging arm, which would frequently seize up through

ingress of road salt. The front forks were also new and fluted in their casting to reduce weight. There weren't any gaiters and the internals worked on the same principle as those in the forks found on the later K6. The mudguard was shortened slightly, and remained chrome-plated, with only one rubber-mounted stay, at the rear.

There was a return to otherwise standard (in other parts of the range) Honda-style chrome headlamp brackets, and larger direction indicators were carried on chrome-plated stems mounted on the upper fork leg. The 'idiot' lights panel remained as on the F1, as did the instruments, although gaining a turquoise-colour finish. The handlebar grips were changed to a softer type still used on certain models today. Switch gear remained the same as on the F1 but the clutch lever housing gained a starter cut-out switch, enabling the bike to be started in gear only if the

lever was pulled in. In the front brake master cylinder a new, taller plastic insert increased the capacity of the reservoir and also allowed the fluid level to be checked without any need for the owner to remove the lid.

The newly black-painted engine came with a fresh design of cylinder head with larger inlet ports (now at 32mm) and inlet valve head diameter up to 34mm; exhaust valves went up 3mm in diameter to 31mm. A new sportier camshaft was fitted and the result of the various changes was a power boost to 73bhp. To cope with the extra power, the crankshaft and its bearings, cylinder head studs, cylinder and clutch springs were all uprated, with the clutch-lifter mechanism subtly altered to retain the light action of the clutch. The carburettors, as before of Keihin manufacture, were a quite different type, with accelerator pump, mated to an air cleaner box which, although at first

Engine output of the F2 was up to 73bhp thanks to various internal changes, including a sportier camshaft.

Styling is unfortunately spoiled on this example of the F2 by period spot lamp and optional Hondastyle crash bar; but fuel tank has artful panelling, colours suggesting a slimmer outline, and Super Sport tank badge is lovely.

F2 silencer is long, tapering and efficient, with meaty-looking business end.

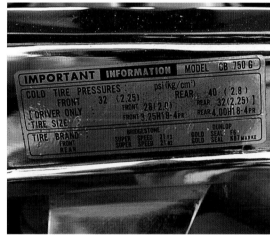

Heavy-duty chain was standard for F2; Marzocchi shocks were a common period fitting. 'Caution' labels on the chain guard relate to drive chain (the need for correct tension and lubrication) and tyres (recommended pressures were higher than for K bikes).

glance appearing unchanged, was modified internally for better breathing and separation of air and oil from the engine breather.

The fuel tank, side panels and tail unit were all of the shape seen on the F1, but the new colours, new trim strips and badges for the tank, the black-finished engine and a completely new four-into-one exhaust system, upswept at the rear, combined to make the F2 look like a completely new model. The suspension at the rear was stiffened to cope with the more sporty nature of the bike, with the rear brake caliper being changed to

match the front ones, instead of carrying on with the heavier Gold Wing type featured on the F1.

My view of the F2? I didn't like it overmuch. Perhaps Honda had tried to make too much of the original design. But the F2 with closer gearing and uprated engine seemed to have lost a relaxed feel; there was now a rather annoying buzziness which gave me, at least, riding along in top, the idea that another gear would have been nice. However, it's true that at the launch of the F2 everybody knew this was only a stop-gap machine, pending arrival of the twin-cam version.

Kick-starter (left) was modified for F series to clear newly rearward-set footrests. View of footrest plate (above) shows rear brake shaft and rear master cylinder. This plate has been chromed; finish should be anodised brushed aluminium. Black paint finish helped to distinguish newly modified 73bhp unit.

Fuel system details. F2 accelerator pump carburettor (above) gave more power than original instrument. Air cleaner (above right) had modified internals for better breathing; revised top rear engine mount plate was introduced at the same time. Fuel tap (right), carburettor plate and inlet rubbers were unique to the F2.

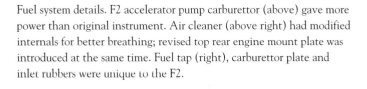

F2 seat has left-hand hinges for convenience of ride-on-the-right Americans and others. Undue loading of the UK-market Hondastyle rack can contribute to steering shimmy.

Wheels on F2 were Honda's new Comstar pattern, with alloy rim and steel spokes. Shown here is F2's twin-disc front braking, high-performing Dunlop Arrowmax rubber and black-painted fork case.

Brake details. Diameter of twin front discs (top) was 20mm less than original K series type. Mounting caliper behind fork legs (top right) reflected mid-'70s worries about unfavourable steering inertia. Front mudguard stay (above) incorporates a hook and rubber grommet on each side to secure brake line. Raised plastic portion of front fluid reservoir (left) gives extra capacity to service two calipers. Rear fluid reservoir (right) is seen with alloy footrest plate, found only on F2 and F3.

Red line on F2 rev counter (above) begins at 9500rpm. Rear-view mirror (above right) is of the correct type.

CB750 F3

Release date 1978 (USA)
Frame number CB750E 2200001
Engine number CB750FE 3100001

This was the last of the F series bikes, and it was sold only in the USA. The changes from the F2 were distinctly minor. The most easily observable clue to F3 identity was a redesigned side cover badge, which still said '750 Four', but in a different italic script from before.

And there was an effective change in the engine's breathing arrangements, to seal any oil spill until the next service. That was about it. End of the road…

F2 front-end details show headlamp assembly, indicator mounting and twin horns. The shot below also clearly shows the new twin disc brake junction, wiring harness clip and the silly Honda badge between the horns.

The Hondamatics Model by Model

CB750A (1976)

Release date 1976
Frame number CB750A 7000001
Engine number CB750AE 7000001

The 1976 CB 750A was the first of the Automatics. It differed in many ways – some of course very fundamental – from the ordinary five-speed models. Leaving the engine and transmission aside for one moment, let me emphasise that it shared many common parts with other models. For instance, wheel rims were from the early spoked-wheel Gold Wing bikes, made by DID in aluminium. They are expensive to replace for the restorer but are an indication of the quality that Honda tried to build into the bike, to help justify its high price. The front mudguard came from the same Gold Wing parts bin (except for a slight bracket change). The fuel tank was the same as the K7's, except for the addition of a fuel gauge float and rheostat. And the frame was very similar

CB750A – this is a 1977 model – allowed motorcycling with only two automatic speeds.

to a K7's, apart from an increase in steering trail. The handlebars were even higher than the normal American market bars, almost 'ape hangers', and the wiring did not go through them as it did with the K series.

The switch gear was as K7 but the instruments were different in that the rev counter was supplanted by a housing with the 'idiot' lights built in plus an illuminated N-L-D (neutral-low-drive) indicator. It also carried the fuel gauge and a parking brake warning light. The seat was heavily sculptured to carry two people a great distance in comfort, with a grab rail built into the rear of the seat. The rear guard was a Gold Wing type, to match the front. Indicators and rear light were of the larger type introduced on the K5 model for the American market. The colours available for the tank and side covers, unique to the Hondamatic, were Candy Antares red and Muscat green metallic. The side panel badges were unique also, with a small square '750' badge and below it 'Hondamatic' in polished alloy lettering. The front brake was the same updated type fitted to the F0,

with the front forks also as on the F0, but with unique-to-the-Hondamatic headlamp brackets that were retained in much the same form through to the last 1978 model. From the side, the 1976 model looked like a K7 equipped with a CB750 F0 exhaust system.

It is difficult to say how, and when, the idea of an automatic motorcycle arrived in the agenda of the Honda Motor Co. The company already had a two-speed semi-automatic transmission, from the N360 car, and with this vital starting point conveniently to hand, many prototype two-wheelers were built. Although the prototypes differed substantially in cosmetics, engine design remained very much the same from the beginning.

As for the engine, imagine a standard five-speed 750 Honda unit chopped off behind the barrels – it was that close to the five-speeder. Head and barrel parts were interchangeable between auto and manual machines. There was a slight drop in compression from the K7's 9.2:1, to 8.6:1, and a softer camshaft (K7, 0°/40°/40°/0°; Auto, 5°/30°/40°/5°). The crankshaft differed only in

Going auto, on a powerful 750, amounted to a travesty of traditional motorcycling for many riders – but was just the job for some.

Engine and carburettors of 1977 CB750A (left and below left). Vacuum throttle opener and extra electrics on tap for Hondamatic help towards stable idle, in neutral or drive. Essentially the CB750A engine was a marginally detuned five-speeder unit. These photographs make it almost impossible to tell whether the engine is an automatic K type or an F.

Main gallery oil plug from a 750 Hondamatic, clearly showing the smooth finish of a die-cast crankcase.

Four-into-two exhaust – giving a single silencer on each side – was unique to 1977 and '78 Hondamatics.

Hondamatic transmission details from 1977 model. Cover and gear pedal (top left): change is of knife-through-butter quality. Neutral arm (top right) is near the gear pedal, which has been removed for clarity. Side stand (left) is connected by rod to the neutral arm. Final view, with gear pedal fitted again (above), shows emergency kick-starter shaft in front, with rubber cover removed for clarity.

Parking brake housing (right) with handbrake cable and warning light wire on 1977 CB750A. Parking brake operates on rear wheel and is required because Automatic cannot be locked in gear when stationary. Detail shows rear brake shoe wear warning arrow (below); brake arm has been strengthened.

Fuel tap on CB750A. One of the de-luxe, or at least new, features of the Hondamatics was a fuel gauge.

American market VIN plate details a CB750A. Month and year of manufacture are recorded in the top right-hand corner of plate.

High-quality DID wire-spoked wheels for the Autos, from the GL1000 Gold Wing, have light alloy rims. Note original-fitment Dunlop tyre.

driving a primary transmission changed from duplex to Hy-vo. The rest of the engine rearwards was unique to the Automatic, with new and bulkier crankcases. In place of the five-speeder's clutch cover, a cover of about twice the size appeared over the Auto's torque converter. The left-hand side was similar except for a stubby gear lever and neutral arm.

The concept of the transmission was very similar to the '50s General Motors Power-glide

system. Power was transmitted to the torque converter, and then to the gears. The gear ranges 1 and D on the 1976 model and L and D on the 1977 and 1978 versions were engaged by means of hydraulically operated clutches. On the shift from neutral into low (0-66mph) a valve opens to engage drive; flick the lever up once again and the valve redirects oil to the second clutch via a gallery system, and 60-105mph drive is engaged. There are no selector forks, sliding gears or

Warning stickers: suddenly motorcycling is a serious business. With lid raised, fuel filler cap and fuel gauge equipment are seen. Striping is very '70s. Hondamatic horn (above), shared with the K6, was of disappointingly low quality.

selector drums. Although it sounds complex, it is in fact extremely simple.

Servicing of the unit is not required, oil is shared with the engine, there is no ATF to play around with, and oil capacity is up from the dry-sump manual model's 3.5 litres to a wet-sump 5.5 litres. If any problem is encountered, removing the torque converter is a simple matter performed in the same way as dealing with an ordinary clutch (albeit with a special tool). Servicing the twin-rotor oil pump – one rotor for the engine (50psi-64psi), another for the transmission (57psi-114psi) – is easy as it can be accessed from the left-hand side, behind the transmission cover, without removing the engine. The hydraulic clutches, coming from a car, are so robust as only to need attention after abuse – when it is true that engine removal and strip-down are called for. Final drive is by 630 O-ring chain, in the normal manner.

The carburettors were of the type fitted to the F2, but of 24mm rather than 28mm, and having a diaphragm, operated by vacuum, to raise the throttle slides slightly when the machine was put into gear, to prevent its stalling.

CB750A (1977)

Release date 1977
Frame number CB750A 7100001
Engine number CB750AE 7100001

The 1977 model was much improved in looks, if only through the addition of tank striping and a unique four-into-two exhaust system. The colours available were Candy Sword blue and Candy Presto red. The grab rail, incorporated in the seat back on the 1976 model, was dropped in favour of

Rear suspension received some revision on 1977 Hondamatic. Note round pillion footrest.

Instruments, seen in 1977 form, say a lot about CB750A's softened character. There is no rev counter for a start, its place taken by 'idiot' lights (including N-L-D transmission indicator) and a fuel gauge. Speedo is now marked in mph and kph – useful for continental touring. Black bolt head covers on handlebar clamp bolts are very tidy. Note also the convenient choke knob and easy-to-use ignition switch with steering lock built in.

CB750A headlamp area on 1977 model: lamp brackets are unique to this model, together with bottom yoke cover.

Rear grab rail, indicators, seat and special fluted rear mudguard (far left) are all as fitted to a 1977 Automatic. Rear lamp and bracket (left) are inscribed, like much else in the electrical line on CB750s, with a distinctly unoriental name – Stanley.

Switchgear on a 1977 Hondamatic. At far left is the rather awkward-to-use dipswitch and direction indicator switch, incorporating halfway position. Right-hand control switch for US-model has no headlamp on/off position because American law decreed lights must be on all the time. Red finish for engine-kill knob was an American idea too.

Large-capacity battery was introduced for the US, where lights had to be on at all times; kick-starter was retained for 'emergencies'.

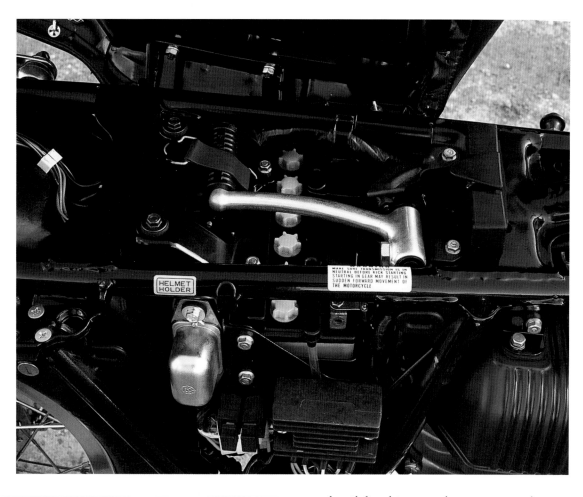

New-type rectifier and one-way diodes were included in electrics for 1977 Auto.

a grab rail fitted in a similar manner to the one used on all the K series bikes since the American K2. The rear direction indicators were attached to the rail, and the seat was made even more plush. There were detail changes to the electrics, mainly doing away with the silly box on the front downtube, and revisions to rear suspension damping.

CB750A (1978)

Release date 1978
Frame number CB750A 7200001
Engine number CB750AE 7200001

The 1978 model Hondamatic was little changed from 1977. Colours were Candy Alpha red and Candy Polaris blue. The easiest change to spot was in the Comstar wheels, which were of the steel and aluminium type used on the F2. Personally, I think these Comstars spoiled the looks of the Hondamatic but by the time the 1978 model had become available few Autos were being sold, in any case, and the model was soon withdrawn. The poor sales of Hondamatics tend to underline the truth that, no matter how adventurous the motor-cyclist may believe himself to be, he is a conservative at heart. I love them and think the best of all the single overhead cam bikes was the 1977 Hondamatic, but I know I am in the minority.

Production Changes

Proud owners of *all* CB750s (which I and friends and acquaintances in the business – all possibly, I'll admit, a tad prejudiced – fondly believe to be en route to 'classic' status) will surely derive much satisfaction in tracing the modifications, however minor, that have been carried out on their fours over the years, from the listing that follows.

Engine changes (E = engine)

CB750E 1000141
Change from 8×80mm hex bolt to 10×82mm hex bolt at rear left-hand side of crankcase, to provide more clamping force next to final-drive shaft.

CB750E 1000219
Change to crankcase set resulting in all crankcase assemblies from engine number 100220 to 1007414 remaining unchanged. Main changes: different oil tube plug, and O ring.

CB750E 1000424
Change to shift drum stopper manufacture to give roller part increased longevity.

CB750E 1001080
Change to rotor setting bolt size (see page 27) from 10mm to 12mm, with change to washer. Change to crankshaft to accommodate new-size rotor setting bolt.

CB750E 1001759
Deletion of clutch plate A necessitated by previous change to clutch outer ring. Deletion of clutch plate stopper ring.

CB750E 1003098
Washers added to bottom of clutch spring deleted at engine number 1005451.

CB750E 1003480
Change to plug cap A and plug cap B.

CB750E 1003527
16-tooth sprocket changed for 17-tooth sprocket.

The first part of this list of production changes includes references to engine numbers. Here is an example from a K6.

Coarse thread at tapered alternator end of crankshaft was introduced at engine number 1001080.

CB750E 1004148
Oil filter bowl changed.

CB750E 1005307
Introduction of set ring for primary drive sprocket outer bearing, with resultant change to bearing.

CB750E 1007414
Change in transmission cover and gasket, to suit fitting to new die-cast cases. Change to clutch cover, adding one extra securing screw with resulting change to clutch cover gasket. Change to sump pan to accommodate newly introduced die-cast crankcase, with gasket change.

CB750E 1007415
Die-cast crankcase introduced with small plate at bottom next to sump. Oil path caps increased from one to three, enabling oil residue to be drained from under crankshaft.

CB750E 1010337
Changes in casting of cam box breather cover, camshaft holder set and to inlet rocker arm shaft.

CB750E 1014995
Change of exhaust valve guide material, valve stem seals on exhaust guides deleted.

CB750E 1017630
Carburettors changed from lightweight cable type to larger cable instruments during production; all bikes before this engine number included in a safety recall.

CB750E 1024073
Change to contact-breaker assembly to accommodate revised breaker plate.

CB750E 1025143
Four washers deleted.

CB750E 1026143
Cylinder change, to accommodate rubber inserts dropping from 22 to 21. Change to rocker arm shaft stopper bolt, thicker nut type introduced. Rubber quietening inserts on cylinder head changed from 12 to 8, slight cylinder head change to accommodate them, cylinder head gasket changed. Change to left rear crankcase cover (front sprocket cover) to accommodate case protector. Change to stopper arm again to accept other shifter part changes. Deletion of tab washer and change of necessary nuts and bolts to complete revision of gear-shift mechanism after complaints of bike dropping out of gear and 'vague' gear shifting. Change to drum stopper plate and gear-shift plate, to accommodate new-style gear-shifting mechanism.

CB750E 1026144
Deletion of bolt for shift drum stopper, bringing in a complete new shaft, resulting in change of shift fork shaft, stopper plate, neutral stopper arm, neutral stopper spring and neutral stopper pivot. Change to final shaft plug to enable chain-oiler to be adjusted – *Ha Ha!* A new final drive shaft fitted, enabling a screw-type adjuster to be fitted to meter oil in place of the earlier non-adjustable type which used a felt plug.

CB750E 1042805
Change made to take stiffer clutch springs.

CB750E 1044805
Change to cam chain tensioner push bar and adjusting bolt; change to inlet rubbers A and B; cylinder head changed again; change to insulated clamping band. Change to breather tube. Change to splined washer at back of clutch centre. Deletion of case protector due to build up of chain grime and addition of final chain-guide rubber. Drive sprocket changed from 17 teeth to 18 teeth.

CB750E 1044812
Carburettors changed from 4 into 1 cable type to push-pull rod operation.

CB750E 1056079
Change to clutch cover to take in revised plate. Deletion of clutch outer ring, now accommodated as part of clutch outer.

CB750E 1060902
Bolt length changed from 6×56mm to 6×60mm.

CB750E 1064092
Change from 6×90mm hex bolt to 6×90mm flange bolt. Change from 6×36mm hex bolt to 6×36mm flange bolt; change on cam chain tensioner housing from 3×36mm hex bolts to 3×6×6×40mm flange bolts. Change from 4×6×22mm hex bolts to 4×6×20mm flange bolts holding clutch springs, with resulting deletion of plain washers. Deletion of 6×56mm hex bolt; replaced by 6×56mm flange bolt holding starter motor in place, with resulting deletion of plain washers. 6×28mm hex bolts changed for 6×28mm flange bolts; 1×6×50mm hex bolt changed for 1×6×50mm flange bolt; with deletion of washers. 6×32mm hex bolts fixing oil pump to crankcases replaced by 36mm long flange bolts. All crankcase hex bolts changed to flange type.

CB750E 1114461
Cylinder head gasket third change.

CB750E 1132192
Change to generator wiring harness to accommodate new-type plug lock.

CB750E 2200000
Cylinder head change for K2.

CB750E 2228679
Change to exhaust valve guides. Cylinder head rubber inserts cut from 8 to 2. Change to head casting.

CB750E 2304500
Change to cylinder-head cover; slight difference in casting. Introduction of Ishino 'sticky' cylinder-head gasket; change to connecting rod bolts, now manufactured by Tikai; slight change to shift drum indents; main jets changed from 110 to 105; changes to cylinder studs for compatability with barrel and head clamping changes.

CB750E 2348902
Change to transmission cover with gear-shift pattern incorporated into casting.

CB750E 2352922
Change to cylinder head gasket, with resultant change to cylinder block to accommodate eight knock pins and O rings.

CB750E 2357330
Cylinder head cover changed; yet another change in casting type.

Frame changes

CB750 1001222
Pillion foot rest bolts changed, corresponding change to no. 1 and no. 4 silencers.

CB750 1002721
Master cylinder oil hose bolt changed from chrome to zinc plate, with rubber boot.

CB750 1003433
Redesigned speedometer and tachometer cushions, with a locating pip incorporated to prevent movement of instruments. Fork top bridge casting strengthened.

CB750 1003480
Modifications to air cleaner element.

CB750 1003951
Front brake hose guide introduced.

CB750 1004007
Air box modified, with rubber mounts sandwiched between air cleaner and bracket; collars introduced in effort to prevent wretched cracking of this extremely expensive item.

CB750 1004149
Exhaust diffusers changed in pattern.

CB750 1011718
Change to throttle grip adjuster, from screw and lock nut type to much-loved spring and thumb screw.

CB750 1013459
Introduction of tyre information sticker on rear mudguard.

Round oil filter bowl was changed in production at frame number 1004148 and by recall at first service.

This type of speedo cable grommet for the front mudguard was fitted from frame number 1015593 onwards.

F2 headstock stamping (top) and VIN plate riveted to front right-hand down tube (above).

CB750 1015593
Introduction of speedometer cable grommet on the front mudguard, with resulting change to front mudguard.

CB750 1017341
Introduction of thick throttle cables on assembly line.

CB750 1019210
Candy gold colours introduced. Introduction of candy gold air cleaner case. Honda winged emblems on side covers changed from gold background to black background.

CB750 1021879
Change to rear chain guard – still in plastic but now extended to alleviate chain lube fling.

CB750 1025845
Introduction of chain guard plate making rear chain guard less prone to deformation and chain-catching; this necessitated a slight alteration to swinging-arm bracketry.

CB750 1026020
Rear brake panel casting changed to take (slightly) redesigned rear-brake anchor pins.

CB750 1026143
Exhaust flanges changed to thicker type.

CB750 1026643
Changes to rear swinging arm bushes.

CB750 1026845
Sprocket side plate introduced. Purpose was to catch rear chain should it jump a sprocket. For K2 version it became full size.

CB750 1030391
Modifications made to air cleaner through bolts in effort to avoid over-tightening of air cleaner sections, resulting in cracked and deformed case. Split pin for each bolt.

CB750 1039119
Front fork stanchions changed. Earlier type had one oil drilling above the top fork pipe stopper ring; now there are two holes. At the same time fork bottom cases changed to carry different size internal circlips and piston stopper rings; plus a change in material of front fork pipe guides.

CB750 1044649
Change to throttle grip to accommodate twin-pull cables. Change to right- and left-hand mirror mounts from type with 6mm dome nut to 'friction' system. Front brake caliper painted

satin black. Front hub changed to thinner type, with resulting change of disc bolts from 8×106mm to 8×102mm. Method of driving the speedometer gear assembly changed at this time, resulting in a different type of speedometer gearbox-drive washer. Changes to back-up rings and oil seal sizes – early oil seals measure 35×46×11mm, later ones are 35×48×11mm – with resulting changes yet again to fork bottom cases and internal circlips, which went from 47mm to 50mm diameter. NOKI type oil seals also introduced at this chassis number. Deletion of original plain silver tank moulding strip, replaced by black strip. Modification to seat catch, with hook introduced to stop the seat accidentally opening. Old square oil tank changed to accommodate new side covers.

CB750 1044650
Introduction of push-pull throttle cable. Master cylinder changed from adjustable lever type to one having rubber insert and lever bush setting plate. Final drive sprocket went from 45 teeth to 48 teeth; rear-wheel hub dampers redesigned.

CB750 1048751
Change to rear suspension springs, including addition of spring seats to stop spring movement.

CB750 1048862
Change to steering stem and bottom yoke to accommodate change in steering lock.

CB750 1055210
Introduction of Candy Garnet brown, Valley green metallic and Polynesian blue metallic. At this stage there was an unprecedented, and never to be repeated, choice of six colour schemes.

CB750 1058490
Speedometer gearbox drive cover changed, with resulting change to O ring.

CB750 1071335
Front brake hose A changed, identifiable by dating ring; hose B also changed at same chassis number.

CB750 1095606
Rear tyre changed in compound and pattern.

CB750 10956605
Front tyre pattern changed.

CB750 1103001
Introduction of famous 'Preserve Nature/Wear a Helmet' sticker on tank top.

Modifying

As is the case with all big-selling motorcycles, in my experience, very few 750s survive in a completely standard condition. This situation is accentuated with a bike that happened to be the fastest of its day.

Julian Grant was an adventurer who rode his CB750 Honda around Australia just after its launch. Falling into a large hole, he managed to smash the crankcase of his machine but somehow carried on to limp into Alice Springs, where he found a man who had just taken delivery of the first CB750 seen in the town. Exercising 'some persuasion' – and one can only speculate that Julian must have been a rare old persuader – he clinched a deal and removed the man's brand new engine, transplanted it into his own machine, and carried on.

Hill-climbing, which is a rather different sport in America from the competition followed in Europe, was something at which the 750 Honda excelled. In the USA, probably the most famous hill-climb outing for the 750 was conducted by one Russ Collins, head of a California tuning firm known, reasonably enough, as RC Engineering. Without doubt, Mr Collins' tuning prowess, as displayed in souped-up CB750s, made him by far the best of all the after-market suppliers.

In 1973 Russ Collins decided to put three 750 engines into a dragbike as a rolling advertisement for his business. This machine had to be seen to be believed. Building it cost Russ $21,000, a massive sum at the time. He took the bike, which he named Atchison, Topeka and Santa Fe, to drag meets around America and wherever he appeared the grandstands were packed. The Honda's 718lb weight, which everybody had sniggered at, was apparently no handicap, and the bike ran a 9.01secs quarter-mile at 164mph on its first shakedown run. Impressively, any customer with an adequate bank account could buy the same parts that Collins used in his own machine and be assured that they would work properly. And anyone with a problem could ring up and speak to Collins himself.

A great shame, however, about this period in the early 1970s is that many owners who customised their bikes into choppers and café racers, in the process threw away what are now sought-after standard parts. Still, there, with the benefit of hindsight, go all of us…

Police bikes

The CB750 was adapted at the Honda factory in Japan for police use. The original police bikes were produced in two variations, for American and Australian markets, painted in white. Much use was made of existing or earlier model parts, combined with standard police-issue paraphernalia such as lights and sirens. The Australian version, for instance, used a modified CB450 headlamp shell widened to accommodate the speedometer, while on the American bike a standard rev counter and speedo were bolted via a bracket to the fork top. A small single seat accommodated the rider, with the pillion seat area given over to the radio box. Crash bars were attached front and rear, and were substantial. An enormous siren was bolted to the right-hand crash bar, being driven by cable from a drum turned by the rear tyre and operated from a lever on the left handlebar. All somehow pleasingly *un*-high-tech. Patrol lamps were bolted to the top of the front crash bars and had blue or red lenses, depending on which market they were designed for. Parts painted white included the lower section of the front forks, headlamp shell and support brackets, fuel tank, side panels, frame, swinging arm, rear shock absorber top shrouds and radio box. The result was quite an eyeful.

The earliest of the police bikes were based on the K1, with engine and frame numbers following a K1 sequence. One or two still exist, and I gather are well cared for by their proud owners.

Racing bikes

It is impossible to make any great sense of the racing CB750s that appeared briefly in 1970: all were factory specials, some with massive drum brakes, some with magnesium crankcases, and so forth. It seems that little or no information on these bikes was ever released by Honda.

Honda had withdrawn from Grand Prix

Standard CB750 K6 cam box (bottom), and CR750-type cam box modified for racing complete with cam carrier hold-down studs.

CR750 racing transmission cover.

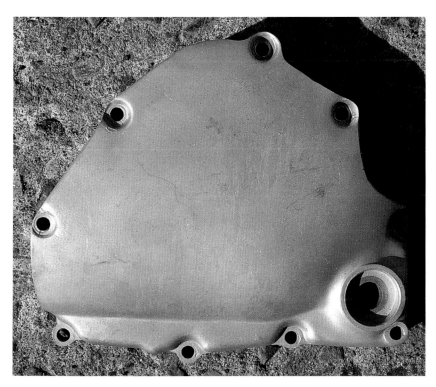

inoffensive 67bhp tourer, be warned – it's an expensive, far-reaching business. Allow me to make free with a few statistics...

As far as the engine is concerned, it's almost entirely a matter of mods to the top end, because down in the crankcase area time and events have shown that the standard set-up can take plenty of extra punishment with impunity. Valve opening must be extended, as follows: inlet should open 20° BTDC (standard camshaft gives 5°), and close 45° ABDC (standard, 30°); exhaust should open 45° BBDC (standard, 35°) and close 20° ATDC (standard 5°). And valve lift has to be increased, to 0.334in for both inlet and exhaust (standard lift is 0.314in inlet, 0.294in exhaust). Special valve springs will be required because the various changes up top should boost maximum revs from 8500 to 10,500rpm. Inlet valve head diameter has to go up to 0.039in, the exhaust valve head to 0.039in also. The standard 28mm Keihin carbs have to go, replaced by 31mm instruments. The standard exhaust system must be replaced by four pipes with attendant megaphones.

Slipper-type pistons giving 10.5:1 compression ratio take the place of the standard 9:1 pistons, with plenty of clearance between piston and bore (0.0019in, compared to the standard clearance of 0.0014in). Although, as indicated, the basic crankshaft assembly requires no help, the same *laissez faire* approach cannot be adopted for the dual primary chains and the cam-drive chain, which have to be judiciously uprated. On the ignition side, the standard alternator is best jettisoned, for an energy transfer system free of the battery, and timing reset at 35° BTDC.

Gear ratios will be a matter of individual taste, of course, but ultimate performance will demand a closer than standard set in the order of, say, top 5.09:1 (standard 5.26:1), fourth 5.95:1 (standard 6.14:1), third 6.70:1 (standard 7.45:1), second 7.86:1 (standard 9.54:1), and first 9.54:1 (standard 13.99:1).

What else? Double discs at the front; alloy wheel rims...perhaps; matched rear suspension units; clip-ons; high-reading tacho...

In addition to all the above, the official, very expensive – at last look, an inlet valve to race spec would set you back £250! – race kit included a new crankshaft assembly, with uprated con rods, bored-out cylinders taking new 61.5mm pistons, modified cam box mounting utilising eight bosses for through bolts securing the cam holders, lightened front mudguard, massive fuel tank, twin leading shoe rear brake, alternative-side gear change mechanisms and full race fairing.

Finally you'll have a 140-150mph road/race bike that might not be humbled by a late '90s Honda CBR600 – a fair testimony to the basic quality of the 750's 30-year-old design.

motorcycle racing in 1967. Really, their return at Daytona in 1970 was a one-off to boost sales of the road-going CB750s. However a race kit, which was approximately twice the price of a new bike, was later made available, to be used by importers and privateers. It comprised a considerable amount of equipment, at a considerable price, which could be fitted to a standard road bike to turn it into an effective 92bhp racer. But if you have ambitions to do something of the sort to your

Buying, Running & Restoring

Right from the beginning, it has to be said that running and riding, or more importantly restoring, a CB750 is a completely different business from dealing with, say, a Triumph or a Harley-Davidson, when all the parts are there to be found at the cost of a telephone call, and the price is easily established. This is not the case with a quarter-century-old Japanese bike. However, it's the initial buying of a CB750 that is the most important part of the process, and after that you'll find that most parts *can* be tracked down to keep one running. As far as I know, all engine parts are still available, but they are not cheap. Chassis components, in particular, can be extortionately

Read all about it. CB750 brochures helped to ensnare potential owners in the '70s, and now, of course, are collectors' items.

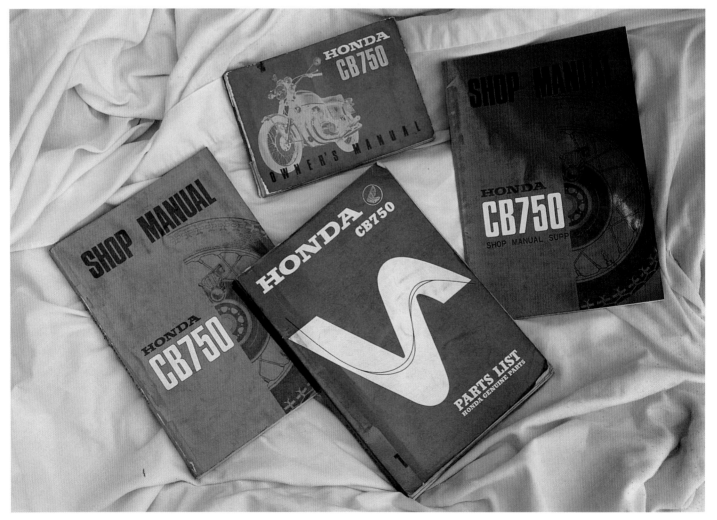

Right-hand carburettor of early CB750: vacuum take-off, idle speed and idle mixture screws await expert attention.

expensive. There are no easy fixes. As with most Japanese machines, the 750 does not take well to sloppy maintenance or give of its best on poorly made pattern parts.

Running and riding, of course, involve much less cash outlay than a restoration. I know people who commute to and in London on CB750s to this day, and they manage to do so economically. As Honda made such a remarkable number of CB750s – a million, give or take a thousand or two, according to some authorities – there are still plenty about all over the world, and as one of their prime plus points was an inherent reliability an example in reasonable condition is still a good bike for someone who wants a classic machine to ride in today's traffic environment. To be fair, and I write as an admirer of all types and makes of machine, wherever they were made, some of the older machines are now not up to constant road use; but the CB750 is a definite exception.

Finding a good one to use every day is not such an easy task. I would have to say 'Don't buy the first one you see'. As mentioned earlier, parts are expensive, which can mean that a bike that is cheaper to purchase than another is not always the better buy. Try to find an original bike with a well-running engine: that's the first line of approach. Usually, a running engine is a good one! But there are exceptions to every rule. Forgetting the matter of mileage covered for a moment, let's take a look at the whole engine. Is it clean? Do all four cylinders work evenly? A good check is to feel

each exhaust pipe for even temperature; or do a compression test, if that is possible. A noisy top-end is a sign that camshaft bearings are worn. This is the first part of the engine to suffer if the oil level is low or the oil hasn't been changed regularly. The remedy will involve a new camshaft, and two new cam carriers, at the very least; plus gaskets to repair. And fitting these means the engine has to be dis-mounted from the frame. A costly exercise. Leave this machine to someone who wants a bike to restore in a big way, and move on to something *quieter*! A leaking head gasket is the next problem. A small weep is acceptable after a run, but over time it will only get worse. I know many owners who have removed the engine to repair a blown head gasket, have used a pattern gasket set – and three weeks later find it's all weeping again. Use a genuine Honda head gasket. This is the only sure cure I know. The gasket will be a Honda updated one and when the engine is warmed up for the first time after repair it glues itself to head and barrel with the heat. So buy it from a Honda dealer or reputable CB750 expert.

There is always a clattering at the bottom end. This is normal. If there's an extremely heavy knocking, though, it means that the accumulated wear of primary chains and/or tensioner, coupled more often than not with badly balanced carburettors, will soon be doing damage. The later models are better here than the earlier ones. If carburettor balancing doesn't quieten things to an acceptable level, then leave well alone as, at the least, a new pair of primary chains will be needed.

Clutches can slip but when they do are easily sorted with a clutch cover gasket and a set of plates. However, trouble here is most unusual, and probably a sign of abuse. Increasing oil consumption usually sets in at around the 40,000-mile mark, although it can begin at any mileage following use with too little oil. The transmission gave some problems in use, but anything amiss here is easily spotted in a test ride, which should be insisted on. A gearbox rebuild is a rare occurrence. Usually, damaged items in a gearbox are bent selectors, resulting from a crash, a lead-footed owner, or a badly repaired change mechanism. Common faults are graunching gears or having gears jump out of engagement…third and fourth being the most likely offenders.

If you find a machine with a good engine, a service on or soon after purchase is always a good idea. If you're doing it yourself, a workshop manual is essential. Start with the engine cold and remove the spark plugs. The middle plugs are the awkward ones to get at: they are buried deep in the cylinder head, and at an angle – so proceed with care. The next part is to check, and adjust, if necessary, valve clearances. The adjusters are under the valve caps (17mm spanner required) and the clearances should be set to 2 thou for the inlet valves and 3 thou exhaust. The contact-breaker points cover has to be removed in order to turn the crankshaft to the T mark on the 1 and 4 cylinder scale, stamped into the face of the advancer. This is the correct position to check 50% of the clearances. One set of valves, either of number 1 cylinder or number 4 cylinder, will be untensioned, ready for checking. Once these are done, ignition timing is next. Set the dwell of the points to 48 degrees and then time 1 and 4 cylinders, followed by 2 and 3 cylinders. Replace the points cover. The last part of engine servicing is to balance the carburettors. The early carburettors are the simplest to balance, but go out of tune more often. They can be balanced with the petrol tank in place. I recommend, on an engine that you don't know, cleaning the pilot jets at this stage. Remove the vacuum take-off screws and fit the vacuum pipes (I find a long thin screwdriver with a dab of grease on the end helps here), fit the vacuum gauges and push up the rubber caps on top of the carbs to get access to the cable adjusters; then unlock the locknuts without disturbing the cable adjusters. Start the bike and warm it up just enough to obtain some kind of idle. Keep revs at 3000 to 4000, which will activate the slides enough to enable you to check how much they are working out of unison. Adjust the cable adjusters to give even readings at 3000 to 4000. Low-speed idle may have now changed but it is easy to restore, using the large idle-speed screws on the carburettor sides. Replace everything, and you should now have a sweet-running engine.

Chassis-wise – things, as we have already said, can become expensive. And in the case of some components, even plenty of money isn't always the answer. However, if what you want is a good, solid runner, and total originality is not important, there's always a way… The front brake, although a revelation in its day, needs to be maintained in tip-top nick to give of its best. In winter it will need plenty of cheap (WD-40) maintenance, to prevent the swinging caliper arm seizing up, together with the pads in their housing. Early-bike forks don't give much trouble, thanks to the fitted gaiters, but oil seals will fail if the gaiters are split. If you are using a machine all year round, I suggest a liberal coating of silicon spray almost everywhere, except on the front disc. A careful eye should be kept on the swinging-arm bushes as well as the rear drive chain.

There are still a few mechanics around from the 1970s, and it is a good idea to try to find one. He will be a fountain of knowledge. One last thing: change the oil at least every 2000 miles! The engine will not put up with infrequent oil changes or low-level oil. And a worn-out engine will consume at least £1000 in parts alone…

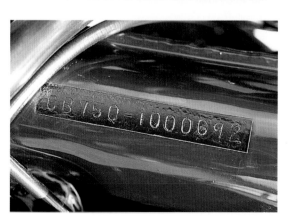

New 'Original Equipment' Bridgestone tyres – much better than their reputation suggested and a rare find today.

Originality should be high among your priorities. This early CB750 should have an early alternator cover, but this later type replaced it following accident damage.

Powder-coating the frame will give it added protection. Mask off the frame number beforehand, as here.

Restoring a Honda CB750

This can be an extremely satisfying project. And of course if the right sort of bike is purchased, it doesn't have to be a bank-busting experience; but it probably will be!

Do bear in mind, however, that if the restoration is done properly the finished machine should last at least another 20 years. Viewed from this perspective, it will be a good investment, for a first-class restoration should mean that the bike will be improved in just about every respect over the original as-bought version. The secret is to buy the best machine you can find (and afford) and not restore it immediately. Ride it for a while to get the feel of what you've bought. A good original 'sandcast' bike is the one which will amount to greatest value at the end, but it will be pricey to buy and restore, and is probably best left to the more affluent collector. But perhaps, of course, that's you? Only 7414 of these were built, so they're rare; a 100 per cent *concours* machine will fetch £8500 or more. Buying one that is in poor condition can cost more than £8500 to restore. Side panels, side panel badges, airbox, seat, original right-hand switches, top yokes, correct master cylinders, discs, fork bushes, correct front guards, tank badges, chainguards and clocks for the 'sandscasters' are now obsolete and very difficult to find. You won't find these bits and pieces at your local swap-meet, unless you are very lucky.

So we can safely say that unless the machine ('sandcast' or K0) is all complete, maybe it's a good idea to look at the later models. Almost all parts for the K3, K4, K5, K6, K7, K8, F0, F1, F2 and F3 are available although, again, they are expensive. A good-condition, all-complete and running K3, for instance, can cost anything from £1000 in America and from £2500 in Europe. That still means excellent value, for the bikes will usually have plenty of life left in them, and with a sympathetic owner will continue to give good service and maintain their value. How long this situation will last is anybody's guess. Supply and demand has been around for centuries, but the market for these Hondas will not go on forever in favour of the buyer.

I remember that a few years ago a Vincent Black Shadow could command £20,000; that's certainly not the case now; call it £12,000 to £15,000. However, imagine buying a new one in 1953, doing 500,000 miles on it, and being able to sell it for £15,000 today!

Of course, as with most desirable objects, heart can and will rule the head. The perfect deal has yet to be made. Set your financial limit. Take someone who really knows CB750s with you when buying – and then, best of all, enjoy some good riding.

For durability, a modern heavy-duty O-ring chain has been fitted to this early bike.

Parts compromises can be frustrating, but sometimes unavoidable. The only type of replacement filler cap now available from Honda is this K6 version. This one incorporates a lock – not standard but a good security measure.

Late-model chain guards, the top one being a standard K6 item and the lower one the component supplied today, made in glass-fibre.

Postscript

Very little official racing was done by Honda after Daytona in 1970. But towards the end of the life of the CB750 the factory began to take an interest in long distance endurance racing. At one stage they used the French Japauto importer as their agent as well as the Honda owned and run Racing Services Corporation to field endurance-racing bikes. RSC was employed too in developing new race machines built up from production components. Of course the racers became more and more specialised, the 'modifications' more extreme – to the extent that twin camshafts appeared – and the direction for the next generation of CB750s was made clear. At this stage Honda brought further development in house, to Japan, while launching the CB750KZ, which followed the styling of the K7 although managing to appear more angular. Equipment was more comprehensive than before: twin discs at the front, Comstar wheels, larger and more powerful lights.

But 10 years had gone by since the appearance of the original CB750, and the other manufacturers had caught up – overtaken – Honda. Suzuki had their GS750, soon enlarged to 1000…excellent bikes with twin camshaft, bullet-proof engines and fine handling. And there was Kawasaki with the Z1, Z900 and Z1000 fours (although perhaps here it was a case of great engines being rather too much for chassis). Yamaha, who I think never seemed to follow any particular trend, always tending to do their own thing, had the XS650 twins which appealed to a certain segment of the motorcycling population addicted to the feel and sound of a vertical twin. Yamaha also, of course, had the XS750 triple which, although rather dodgy in its first year, became very reliable, and always had a distinctive sound – and shaft final drive, which was one in the eye for Honda. One of the drawbacks associated with the CB750 was the woefully short life of tyres and chains; many people were fed up with changing these on a far too regular basis, and so the Yamaha's shaft drive was a great selling point. I think the dohc CB750 KZ was a rather weak attempt by Honda to follow up on the single-over-head-cam version. Market share was lost. The best thing Honda did at the close of the '70s was to introduce the six-cylinder CBX 1000.

It took Honda another 12 years to produce anything like the CB750, and that one was (is) the Fireblade, or CB900RR. However, it is debatable whether this one is as much of an all-rounder as the sohc 750 was in its day.

In my view, it's doubtful that a motorcycle will ever be built in the future that will have the impact of the CB750. This is a bike that will always hold a very important place in the history of motorcycling and in the hearts of owners.

Bibliography

Soichiro Honda: The Man and His Machines Sol Sanders
Honda Motor: The Men, The Management, The Machines Tetsuo Sakiya
Honda: The Early Classic Motorcycles Roy Bacon
Honda Roland Brown
CB750 Peter Shoemark
Cycle World on Honda 1968-1971
Honda Mick Walker
Honda Mick Woollett and others
Honda UK Story Eric Dymock
Japanese Motorcycles: The Machines and the Men Behind Them Cyril Ayton

Specialists

John Wyatt's Rising Sun Restorations, Unit 10D Marston Moor Business Park, Tockwith, York YO26 7QF Telephone: 01423 358004 Fax: 01423 359660

P. F. K. Ling Ltd, Honda Parts Centre, Mendham Lane, Harleston, Norfolk IP20 9DW. Tel: 01379 853213 Fax: 01379 854373

David Silver Spares, Unit 14, Masterlord Industrial Estate, Station Road, Leiston, Suffolk Telephone: 01728 833020

Your local Honda dealer

Clubs

The Honda Owners Club (GB), Membership Secretary, 61 Vicarage Road, Ware, Hertfordshire SG12 7BE